West Midlands PTE
Buses and Trolleybuses

Malcolm Keeley

Ian Allan
PUBLISHING

First published 2009

ISBN 978 0 7110 3422 8

© Malcolm Keeley 2009

Published by Ian Allan Publishing
an imprint of Ian Allan Publishing Ltd, Hersham, Surrey, KT12 4RG

Printed in England by Ian Allan Publishing Ltd, Hersham, Surrey, KT12 4RG

Code: 0910/B

Visit the Ian Allan Publishing website at
www.ianallanpublishing.com

Front cover: Heavily outnumbered by Daimler Fleetlines were the 11 Metro-Cammell-bodied Leyland Atlanteans inherited by the PTE from Birmingham City Transport. The first of these, 3230, had begun life in 1960 as a Leyland demonstrator and is seen on 15 June 1973 tackling the brief climb away from Camp Hill before making the long descent to Birmingham's Markets Quarter.

Back cover (upper): The biggest upheaval to the PTE's operations came at the end of 1973 with the takeover of Midland Red's local services. Nowhere would this be more apparent than at Dudley, filled by the red buses that were now destined to become blue and cream. With a Leyland National (135) peering between them, BMMO D9 No 4957 and S17 No 5758 dominate this view of the bus station on 30 April 1974. The Midland Red buses came in three shades, but these are all in NBC poppy red.

Back cover (lower): The PTE fleet was further enlarged in April 1974 with the takeover of municipal operations in Coventry. From 1955 to 1963 Coventry bought Metro-Cammell 'Orion'-bodied Daimler CVG6 buses, and many of these passed to the PTE. Seen passing through picturesque Allesley Village on 6 May 1975, No 271Y, a 1959 delivery, would run until 1977.

Previous page: In the PTE's early days a number of ex-Birmingham Guys were transferred to Walsall, but 2564 ultimately returned to the South Division, being beautifully repainted at Walsall beforehand: the khaki roof and the line beneath the lower-saloon windows were retained, and the Guy Indian head survived, carefully repainted silver. It is seen entering Broad Street on 22 May 1973, providing one of the lunchtime extras between the City centre and the many offices at Five Ways.

Introduction

THE TRANSPORT ACT 1968, introduced by Harold Wilson's Labour Government, prescribed the creation in major conurbations of Passenger Transport Executives. Their task was 'to secure or promote the provision of a properly integrated and efficient system of public passenger transport to meet the needs of that area …'. Each PTE would be managed by transport professionals carrying out the policies of a Passenger Transport Authority comprising elected representatives from the local authorities.

The new West Midlands Passenger Transport Executive was led by Director General Fred Lloyd, formerly Chief Commercial and Planning Officer of the London Transport Board and thus experienced in a single transport entity serving a large conurbation. West Midlands was the first operational PTE, absorbing the municipally-owned buses of Birmingham, Walsall, West Bromwich and Wolverhampton with effect from 1 October 1969.

The largest contribution to the new WMPTE came from Birmingham City Transport, accounting for around two-thirds of the new 2,100-strong fleet and 8,500 employees. WMPTE buses would adopt the blue and cream colours of Birmingham City Transport but with a brighter (Oxford) blue.

Work towards an integrated transport network proceeded, and an agreement for significant control over the local services of British Rail was signed in January 1972. Buses between the towns, however, were generally run by Midland Red, by now a subsidiary of the National Bus Company, which had been created under the same Transport Act. Negotiations to achieve integration led to the purchase of Midland Red's local services in December 1973, bringing in a further 1,400 employees and 413 buses. The takeover meant that integration of operators' services could begin in earnest.

There followed a period of considerable revision and development of the region's bus and train services as the integration brief was pursued. This was slightly hampered by a revision of the PTE boundaries. The boundaries as originally drawn were based, logically, on 1960s transport studies but were now altered to match those of the new West Midlands county, created in 1974. This needlessly included Coventry, along with its municipal fleet of 309 buses, but excluded from the PTE area notable satellite towns and dormitory areas, among them Bromsgrove, Cannock and Redditch, the last a massive new town absorbing many people continuing to look towards the conurbation.

The PTEs were much more than just bus operators, and WMPTE invested heavily in bus stations. It also believed that its employees should enjoy good working conditions and rebuilt bus garages that, in turn, assisted the maintenance of the fleet. Other significant expenditure was on bus/rail interchanges and local rail development, including introduction of the Cross City line. However, for many years the rail system remained heavily dependent on trains dating from the late 1950s. Plans for a light-rail system were in hand by the mid-1980s, but to date there exists only the single route introduced in 1999.

The election in 1979 of Margaret Thatcher's Conservative Government brought massive change to the bus industry. Subsidies designed to modernise it were reduced, the Metropolitan County Councils were disbanded, and in 1985 a new Transport Act was passed. Among other things this decreed that the majority of Britain's bus services should be deregulated and that PTEs should no longer be directly involved in providing them. Thus with effect from 26 October 1986, 'Deregulation Day', WMPTE's bus operations were transferred to a new 'arm's length' operator, West Midlands Travel (itself subsequently privatised), and this forms a convenient end date for this book.

To this day the PTE, in conjunction with the Passenger Transport Authority (PTA), continues all the other integration functions such as sourcing socially necessary bus services (by means of competitive tendering), administering the split of concessionary fares, maintaining bus stations and shelters and managing a contract with the local privatised successor to British

Many types of bus helped out at the garages taken over from Midland Red. A one-off from the Wolverhampton Corporation fleet, 19N had been the prototype for that concern's many forward-entrance Guy Arab 30-footers. A 68-seater Mk IV new in 1958, it was the only one with Burlingham coachwork, very similar to bodies supplied on Leyland chassis to Ribble. Typically soft Guy springs cause it to roll as it negotiates Summer Row, Birmingham, while working from Oldbury garage on 29 March 1974. It would be withdrawn later that year.

Rail. Understandably, there was considerable public confusion between WMPTE and West Midlands Travel, as a result of which the PTE re-branded itself as Centro.

* * *

Having read what had happened after the creation of London Transport in 1933, I realised from the start that there would be a very interesting period of change before a sea of uniformity spread over the whole area. This was true for around a decade, and I made sure I covered as much as I could photographically. No apologies are offered for the number of pictures taken in Walsall in the early days: the collection of vehicles taken over and transferred there made it the place to be, and one had to flit from one terminus to another to keep up with developments. The influx of Bristol VRTs ultimately reduced this interest, but the Midland Red takeover made Dudley bus station a new centre of attention. Much of the interest lay in acquired buses operating in the 'wrong' town, and this is something I have endeavoured to highlight in this book.

Unless otherwise credited the pictures are my own, but sincere thanks are due to the other photographers, along with The Transport Museum, Wythall, for their loan of precious colour transparencies. Thanks go also to Paul Gray, who as usual has striven valiantly to weed out errors factual and grammatical. My principal source of information was *West Midlands*, written by myself and published in 1988 by Capital Transport. I am also indebted to the PSV Circle and The Omnibus Society for the detailed information provided in their WMPTE fleet history (ref: 2PD13).

Malcolm Keeley
Shirley, Solihull
August 2009

Walsall — the place to be in 1970! Two very different Park Royal-bodied Leyland PD2 Titans taken over from Walsall Corporation compete for attention in Bradford Place on 24 March. No 203L was one of three surviving RTLs (with preselector gearboxes) of the five purchased by Walsall from London Transport in 1959, while 238L represents the 50 full-front buses delivered to Walsall in 1951, half based on Guy Arab chassis and half, as here, on PD2/1, with the usual synchromesh gearbox.

Above: Birmingham became the South Division of the new PTE. If there was one word to sum up BCT's vehicles it was quality, encapsulated in its superb livery of dark blue and cream. Along with high standards of design and construction came a maintenance regime to match. Dented panels were not tolerated — new damage was immediately obvious — so driving standards were above average. The oldest buses still around at the time of takeover were the Park Royal-bodied Leyland Titan PD2s delivered in 1949/50, of which Nos 2223 and 2229 are seen in June 1969 at the Baldwin, southern terminus of the cross-city 90/91 service from Pheasey. Both

were then allocated to Yardley Wood garage and returning there after the evening peak, the driver of 2223 having erroneously wound up the wrong destination. PD2s were cool runners, so, to avoid complaints from chilled drivers, Yardley Wood never used them after the evening peak following receipt of its first Fleetlines. Only 2229 ran for the PTE, but 2190/1, 2202/9/11/3/4/8/23/4/6/8 were received as recently withdrawn buses. To minimise the number of drivers being taught on manual gearboxes 2229 had been moved to Perry Barr garage by the time of the PTE takeover. It lasted until November 1969 and did not receive PTE fleetnames.

Left: Two 1950 Crossleys, 2471 and 2505, with bodies built by Crossley itself, survived to run for the PTE, albeit not lasting long enough to receive new fleetnames. Being manual-gearbox too, the Crossleys were also allocated to Perry Barr garage at the time of takeover. Perry Barr contributed to the 5 route, and 2471 and 3123, also Crossley-bodied but on Daimler CVG6 chassis, are seen descending New Street in May 1969.

*Right:*The first new buses received by the PTE, in 1969/70, were Daimler Fleetlines with Park Royal bodies, ordered by Birmingham and Wolverhampton. Like Birmingham's previous batch of Fleetlines they had the additional centre exit doors. A fatal accident involving one of the first batch of centre-exit buses had caused a timelag device to be fitted, preventing engagement of a gear for several seconds after the centre door had closed, so they were actually slower at stops than single-door buses. The bodies were built to Park Royal's new larger window style and were 33ft long, giving rise to their 'Jumbo' nicknames. The first 15 carried Birmingham's blue, the first two having coats of arms. No 3882 is seen on service 18 at The Valley on 10 October 1969.

Left: A 25% grant was available from the Government for buses suitable for one-man operation. As the PTE settled in, the standard livery evolved over the delivery of the 124 'Jumbo' buses. Seen working its way through the conversion of Suffolk Street into part of the Queensway inner ring road in August 1970, 3914 was one of the fleet for Birmingham's Bristol Road services and featured WMPTE's Oxford blue on its Birmingham-style livery, with black lines separating the colours. The 'Jumbo' bodies soon developed problems; 3914 and 3947 quickly had plain glass fitted in the front upper-deck windows to try to reduce movement in the front dome, but the others retained their opening vents.

*Below:*No 3936 turns at the Northfield terminus of service 20 in June 1970. Nos 3935 onwards had introduced a simplified livery with black lining retained only to separate the khaki roof from the cream. Although the Wolverhampton part (3980-4004) of the combined contract had been revised to be the same as the Birmingham buses there were detail differences (notably in the design of hopper vents fitted), presumably because parts had already been ordered.

Left: While Birmingham's buses did not need renumbering, those of the new North Division — Walsall, West Bromwich and Wolverhampton — duplicated each other, so a suffix letter, representing the last letter of the former operator, was added. West Bromwich was quick off the mark with 1962 Daimler CVG6-30 No 240H in PTE livery; this photograph is believed to have been taken on 1 October 1969. *Graham Harper*

Left: Each West Bromwich Corporation bus soon had its fleetnames painted out and PTE legal address substituted, as seen here on 1965 Daimler CVG6-30 No 259H. The coat-of-arms lasted a little longer, pending arrival of the new fleetname and logo, applied using self-adhesive stickers in the appropriate background colour for each vehicle. Both this and the previous photograph were taken in Paradise Street, West Bromwich. *Graham Harper*

Left: The simplified livery was introduced on repaints of rear-engined Birmingham buses in October 1969. Birmingham's Tyburn Road Works applied the new blue to 3629 and then, curiously, reapplied BCT blue to rear-engined buses for the next few months while applying the new shade to most front-engined types. Daimler Fleetline/ Park Royal 3423 of 1964, freshly repainted in BCT blue, is seen in Victoria Square on 17 October 1969.

Right: An interesting November 1969 shot of ex-Walsall 65-seat Daimler CVG6/Metro-Cammell 62L, new in 1963, in the same style of WMPTE blue as that worn by 3935 etc. This includes the black line applied by BCT to separate the khaki roof from the cream whenever there was no panel strip and thus always to be found on its frameless dome buses. BCT fleet numbers complete the disguise. One can imagine the conversation going something like: "Instead of painting that thin line fourteen feet up, wouldn't it be more sensible to paint it around the middle and break up all that cream? And while we're about it, can't we have bigger fleet numbers back instead of these eye-test Birmingham ones?" And so it came to pass. *Royston Morgan*

Left: Fleetline/Metro-Cammell 3695 of 1967 was one of the last to receive the drab arrangement of BCT blue without lines, as the finalised livery and lettering was adopted in March 1970, partway through repainting this batch of 50 buses. The 44 used to be the principal bus service along the Warwick Road, branching off at the city boundary with Olton, in Solihull, to terminate at Lincoln Road North. Certain journeys turned short on Saturdays and during the peaks at Olton Boulevard East, where 3695 is seen on Saturday 9 October 1971.

Right: It was not unusual, once the evening peak was cleared from Cadbury's Bournville Works, for one of Selly Oak's single-deckers from service 27 to finish its day with a trip on the main Bristol Road. The livery applied to AEC Swift 3671, seen leaving John Bright Street in July 1971, was possibly unique on a single-decker, combining PTE blue with BCT's generous black lining.

Right: Wolverhampton had been an enthusiastic operator of trolleybuses, but all had gone by 1967. A legacy of the trolleybus-replacement programme was the survival of some motor buses well past their sell-by date. Nothing wrong with old buses, but the bodies were perhaps not of the best construction and were indifferently maintained. The green of the older buses was relieved by yellow in a much greater (and arguably more attractive) proportion. No 540N was a preselector Guy Arab III with Park Royal body, and 518N a Daimler CVG6 bodied by Brush, both new in 1950. No 518N was withdrawn by the PTE in 1969, but 540N lasted until 1971.
Royston Morgan

Below: Forty-six operational trolleybuses came with the Walsall fleet and were the only such vehicles to be operated in normal service by a PTE. They were heavily outnumbered by more than 2,000 motor buses, so it was easy for such a large organisation to sweep them away. All the trolleybuses save Nos 345 and 856 had their Walsall insignia painted out. None received PTE fleetnames or suffix letters to their fleet numbers — they did not duplicate anything, nor were they likely to run in other areas. A considerable proportion of the trolleybus fleet was second-hand, Walsall having taken advantage of systems' closing down elsewhere. The PTE thus acquired seven 1950 Sunbeam F4 trolleybuses with Park Royal bodies that had originated in Ipswich. Six, including No 345, seen here on 20 September 1969, were withdrawn as part of the first stage of the trolleybus replacement, but 353 survived until the final day. No 876 was a 1950 BUT 9611T acquired from the Grimsby-Cleethorpes system, its traditional rear-entrance 54-seat Northern Coach Builders body being extended to 30ft and rebuilt with a forward entrance before entry into service. There were four of these, three being treated to this drastic rebuilding.

Above: As the 'Jumbo' Fleetlines arrived, Metro-Cammell-bodied Daimler CVD6 buses dating from 1951 became surplus in Birmingham. Ten (2626/30/2/40/1/3-5/7/9) were sent to Wolverhampton in November 1969 to replace the most decrepit buses there. Wolverhampton staff, misunderstanding the purpose of the letter suffixes, gave them 'N' suffixes. Some later moved on to West Bromwich and Walsall, but 2645, having picked up an advertisement contract for a local firm on its illuminated offside panel, remained at Wolverhampton and is pictured entering Queen Street, with handsome buildings in Pipers Row as a backdrop, in May 1970. The advertising contract was taken over in September 1970 by a slightly later CVD6, 2762, itself replaced by a similarly equipped Guy, 3056, in July 1971.

Below: No route mileage was lost upon the first stage of the trolleybus replacement on 16 February — motor buses simply took over certain workings. Among trolleybuses withdrawn at this time were 874, the ex-Grimsby-Cleethorpes BUT/Northern Coach Builders that had not been extended, and all remaining ex-Hastings 1947 Weymann-bodied Sunbeam W vehicles, including 306, with more of that white window rubber.

Above: The next buses to be transferred from the South Division to the North were 30 newly overhauled Guys with Metro-Cammell bodies, built in 1950/1. Nos 2564-80/2-4/6-93/5/6 were transferred between January and March 1970 and assisted in the first stage of the replacement of Walsall's trolleybuses, on 16 February. However, a few went first to Wolverhampton, where preselector Guys were more familiar than at Walsall, not reaching their intended destination until the second and final stage of trolleybus replacement. A survivor of the first stage was 342, a 1951 Sunbeam F4 with Brush bodywork, seen loading for an enthusiasts' tour, with two ex-Birmingham Guys behind. It had been lengthened to 30ft, increasing its seating capacity from 56 to 65, and fitted with new windows mounted in General Manager Ronald Edgley Cox's favoured white rubber, re-entering service in this form in 1965. *Graham Harper*

Above: Wolverhampton overpainted the Corporation name and coat-of-arms before applying the new self-adhesive fleetnames, and AEC Renown 184N, one of five new in 1966, was still in anonymous state in May 1970. Construction of the Nottingham-styled 72-seat bodywork was begun by Weymann, but, when its factory in Addlestone closed, they were completed by the other partner in MCW, Metro-Cammell. The five had semi-automatic gearboxes and were later transferred to Walsall to join the AEC Regent Vs there.

Left: Wolverhampton's paint shop struggled with the concept of a khaki roof on frameless-dome buses. Its initial solution was to restrict the khaki to the middle panels only, but this did not meet with approval. Traditional Wolverhampton gold fleet numbers were still applied at this time. No 163N, a 1965 Guy Arab V with 72-seat Metro-Cammell bodywork, loads at the 59 terminus in Exchange Street, Wolverhampton, in May 1970.

Above: Three Guys outside Cleveland Road garage, Wolverhampton, in May 1970. Its elegant Roe body blighted by a Strachans front dome, fitted after accident damage, 1953 Arab IV No 572N demonstrates the finalised WMPTE livery with one relief band in blue but, at the time of its repaint, still using the existing style of Wolverhampton fleet numbers. Behind are respectively Mk V and Mk IV Guy Arabs, wearing the liveries favoured by Wolverhampton Corporation for newer and older members of its fleet.

Below: An attractive livery based on Birmingham's 1967 single-deckers was applied to buses with a beading strip splitting the lower panels. Leyland Royal Tiger PSU1/13 No 801L, new to Walsall Corporation in 1952 with Leyland's own bodywork, was one of the first to wear the scheme — but not for long, for it was scrapped in 1970. Impressive spotlamps! *Paul Roberts*

Above: New to Walsall in 1956, 826L was the first of a batch
of 15 Daimler CVG6 buses with 66-seat Willowbrook bodies
built to the lowest height possible while retaining highbridge
seating layout, hence the squat appearance. It was an early
repaint into PTE livery and carried the small black BCT
numbers; the thin blue midriff stripe was adopted from
around February 1970. Walsall continued to paint the front
bulkheads completely blue for a couple of years. Seen in
Walsall's main St Paul's Street bus station in August 1971,
826L would be retired in 1972, but most of the batch would
survive until 1974.

Below: Another Daimler entering service in Walsall in 1956
was this one-off. No 401L was a CVG5 with the smaller
(7-litre) Gardner 5LW engine and a body built by the
Corporation itself on Metal Sections frames. As well as being
to the earlier 7ft 6in width it was exceptionally tall, giving it a
galleon-type presence and restricting it to the 37/38 Walsall–
Darlaston–Wednesbury circulars. Seen at Darlaston in June
1970, it would be retired the following year. Walsall's fleet
was scruffily maintained — that bent grille would have given
any BCT engineer a fit!

Above: West Bromwich's superb livery was justly famed, if not (by Birmingham standards) frequently reapplied. This gave its buses an air of genteel neglect, but they were, in fact, well maintained. The frugality was forgivable, because West Brom enjoyed the lowest fares in the area, and the PTE had to maintain a modified fare scale in the town for some years. The oldest operational West Bromwich vehicles were survivors of the 20 Daimler CVG6 buses with rather grand Weymann bodies. The livery and flared panels gave them an antique appearance, but they were new in 1952, roughly comparable to Birmingham's 27xx Daimlers. No 166H is seen in High Street, West Bromwich, in May 1970.

Below: Most of West Bromwich's buses were concealed-radiator Daimler CVG6 vehicles with Metro-Cammell 'Orion' bodies. Small batches were taken most years from 1955 to 1965, the design gradually evolving. Pictured at Dartmouth Square in May 1970, 209H dated from 1957, being one of the last batch with preselector gearboxes. The 1958 buses were the first 30-footers and introduced semi-automatic gearboxes as standard; No 222H, following, was a 1959 example. The 1960 and 1964 batches were built to the earlier length of 27ft.

Right: To BCT staff 'Standard' meant a traditional 54- or 55-seat rear-entrance double-decker, regardless of whether the bus had an exposed radiator or a 'New Look' concealed front. It did not mean much in engineering terms, for quite a lot was not transferable between manufacturers. 'Standard' differentiated the pre-1954 stock from 'Large Capacity Buses', represented by the Daimler Fleetline and Leyland Atlantean double-deckers. In time the term 'Standard' caught on throughout the PTE, although, given that by then only 'New Look' examples remained, this caused some confusion among enthusiasts. There were non-standard 'Standards', including two Crossley-bodied Daimler CVG6 buses with 'Manchester' fibreglass front ends, this being a design adopted by Daimler from the late 1950s to improve nearside visibility. Wearing a brand-new coat of paint, 2799, of Liverpool Street, climbs the Bull Ring on 25 June 1970. Fortunately the broad blue bands were retained on these buses, although the fine line below the lower-saloon windows was not. The large fleet numbers, available in black or cream, had been introduced in March throughout the organisation and in size were more akin to those employed by the municipalities swallowed by the North Division. The other 'Manchester'-front bus, 2880, never received PTE livery.

Right: The Metro-Cammell body of 1952 Guy 2926 was rebuilt in 1956 as a 57-seater with angled staircase and fitted throughout with hopper ventilators. It was thought in 1969 that buses would need a second fog lamp to meet incoming regulations; equipping began with accident-damaged 'Standards' and by working through the garages in alphabetical order, with the result that Acocks Green's stock, including 2926, pictured climbing the Bull Ring in July 1970, was dealt with first. Cotteridge and Coventry Road no longer had any 'Standards', so work had begun on Harborne's by the time it was learned that only the newest buses needed a second fog lamp.

Above: The next new vehicles to arrive, in the spring of 1970, were 4005-12, Daimler Fleetlines with Northern Counties bodywork but matching the 33ft length and dual-door layout of the Park Royal-bodied examples. Seven were a West Bromwich order, while the eighth was a replacement for the 125th Fleetline/Park Royal, retained by Daimler and exported to Johannesburg, South Africa. All eight went to West Bromwich, where placing the 'via' point in the upper destination aperture was normal. The 90 Wolverhampton–West Bromwich route, operated jointly by the two towns, contributed to one of the PTE's earliest significant route developments: with effect from 28 February 1971 it was combined with overlapping Wednesbury–Birmingham journeys on route 75 (a joint West Bromwich/Birmingham operation) to create an important new route, 79, which for the first time brought Birmingham- and Wolverhampton-based buses into each other's territory. Wolverhampton used its big Guys from the outset, West Bromwich and Birmingham's Hockley garage initially continuing to use small double-deckers, but loadings dictated conversion to higher-capacity buses, effected from 3 May 1971. *Royston Morgan*

Bottom left: Bodybuilder Metro-Cammell-Weymann was alarmed by the rapid concentration of British bus-chassis manufacturing — and to some extent bodybuilding — into the British Leyland empire. Fearing it could be squeezed out, it worked in partnership with Scania of Sweden to develop complete vehicles — something it used to do with the old Leyland Motors, producing most notably the world-beating Olympic. Metro-Scania demonstrator VWD 452H passes through Bournville Green on 6 June 1970 while on loan to WMPTE at Selly Oak garage.

Right: A Ford R226 with 53-seat Willowbrook body, 4028 was received following an order placed by Wolverhampton. It was the first of its type to be fitted with a semi-automatic gearbox, and its experimental nature meant that it was retained by Ford as a demonstrator, registered HVW 798H instead of TOC 28H as had been originally intended. It entered service with the PTE in the summer of 1970, being seen in August in Brunel Street, Birmingham, and ran from Selly Oak garage until February 1971.

Above: Nos 4013-27 were further dual-door Northern Counties-bodied Fleetlines, albeit reverting to 30ft length. They met an order placed by Walsall and included access flaps for Mr Edgley Cox's giant vacuum-cleaner; this device was strapped to the back of a withdrawn bus, the idea being that the 'scrapper' would be sold with all the rubbish accumulated within! Delivered between August and October 1970, they permitted the withdrawal of Walsall's last trolleybuses, on 3 October. No 4027 is seen at the Cenotaph in Bradford Place in August 1972 on the long Dudley–Stafford service, worked jointly with Midland Red; from December 1973 the Stafford section would be worked exclusively by Midland Red.

Below: The second and final stage of trolleybus replacement was implemented on 3 October 1970. Seen in Bloxwich Lane shortly before the end, 867 was a Sunbeam F4A with 70-seat Willowbrook bodywork, one of 22 such vehicles delivered to Walsall in the period 1954-6. *Derek Williams, courtesy Graham Harper*

Above: The elderly 54-seaters transferred from Birmingham did not have the Walsall ex-trolleybus routes entirely to themselves; from November 1970 Walsall began to collect ex-Wolverhampton Guy Arab V 72-seaters, and these were also favoured for the ex-trolleybus routes. Wolverhampton had so few vehicles suitable for the extension of one-man operation that the transfers were often exchanges for Walsall Fleetlines, many continuing to operate in Walsall blue in their new home. The Guys, with their semi-automatic gearboxes, were yet another variant for the Walsall engineers to cope with. Weymann-bodied 89N, one of a batch which when new in 1963 had replaced some of Wolverhampton's trolleybuses, loads at Blakenall, Walsall, in August 1971.

<table>
<tr><td>ᴡᴍ</td><td>UNTIL SATURDAY, FEBRUARY 20th
Fares will remain in shillings and
old pence.

Please pay in old coinage
or if not possible in
2½p 5p 7½p or 10p units</td></tr>
<tr><td>DECIMAL
FARES</td><td>ON SUNDAY, FEBRUARY 21st
Revised decimal fares commence
Please pay in new pence

CORRECT FARE PLEASE
AT ALL TIMES</td></tr>
</table>

Right: New invention? Not really. Among Birmingham's non-standard 'Standards' were six constant-mesh-gearbox Guys, 2995-3000, which would have been much more at home in Walsall than among all the preselectors at Washwood Heath garage. After four were withdrawn in July 1971 survivors 2995/6 passed to Walsall, where 2996 is seen in June 1972 with a dented front cowl — never allowed under BCT. The writer rode on the ex-Birmingham Guys after a few months at Walsall and was shocked at the dingy interiors. The benefit of Birmingham's periodic interior special cleans was all too clear.

Left: West Bromwich bus station was opened on Sunday 25 March 1971. Here Daimler CVG6/Metro-Cammell 178H of 1955 has just arrived, while standing in the parking area is sister bus 183H, with a different style of front vents. Compare the liveries and choose your preference. *Graham Harper*

Above and left: Withdrawn 1954 Guy Arab IV buses at Wolverhampton in November 1971. No 584N was one of seven with very early examples of Metro-Cammell's lightweight 'Orion' body, while 585N was a one-off in the fleet, having a body built by Guy itself on Park Royal frames. Alongside 584N is ex-Birmingham Guy 3056, at Wolverhampton to fulfil a contract with its offside illuminated advertisement panel; it had been a very early repaint into PTE livery, in November 1969, when BCT-style fleet numbers were still being applied.

Above: The PTE soon developed its own standard bus, built to the more manœuvrable 30ft length, fitted with a single entrance door and a revised destination layout, and suitable for one-man operation. The design was, of course, eligible for the Government's New Bus Grant. However, the 'Jumbos', built to the taller (14ft 6in) of the two permitted Bus Grant height dimensions, had been too high to pass under certain bridges. Not wishing to resort to the lower dimension of 13ft 8in, the PTE persuaded the Ministry of Transport to accept an intermediate height of 14ft 2in. The first such vehicles entered service in July 1971, and around 1,200 to this general specification would be received by 1979. Continuing the preferences of the constituent fleets, the majority were Daimler Fleetlines, Park Royal or MCW constructing most of the bodies. There was also a final order for seven buses, originally intended for West Bromwich, that had Northern

Counties bodywork, these entering service at Walsall in October 1971. Nos 4029-35 did their best to conform to the new PTE standard, but Northern Counties, body supplier to Walsall for some years, would fail to feature in any subsequent Fleetline orders. On 4 November 1972 No 4030 was photographed in Bradford Place, Walsall, alongside Park Royal-bodied 4104, also then working at Walsall. These were among the first new buses to be delivered with a cream roof, this having been adopted as standard from the autumn of 1971, including repaints of earlier buses. Significant exceptions among the latter were those with khaki roofs, which if repainted at South Division's Tyburn Road Works would almost inevitably retain this feature. Upon the delivery of new Bristol VRTs to Walsall in March 1975 4029-35 finally made it to West Bromwich to help with increased one-man operation there.

Left: From 1 December 1971 the Government grant increased from 25% to 50% for new buses suitable for one-man operation, which now accounted for 30% of the PTE's mileage. Metro-Cammell took a little longer to change to cream roofs, Fleetlines 4171-5, entering service in February 1972, being the last buses delivered with khaki. Miller Street's 4165 loads at the 42 terminus in Lower Bull Street in April 1974.

Above: Many of the earliest standard PTE Fleetlines went to garages operating the Birmingham–West Bromwich–Dudley/Wolverhampton services, allowing these to be converted to OMO. A considerable number of Daimler CVG6 buses thus became surplus at West Bromwich, and those delivered between 1960 and 1964 (228-32/4-49/53-8H) were transferred to Walsall by the end of 1971, all repainted in PTE livery. They particularly settled on the ex-trolleybus services, causing the ex-Birmingham Guys there to adopt a more interesting lifestyle, working peak-hour journeys on a wide variety of services. Many ex-Walsall buses were withdrawn, several of Walsall's ex-Birmingham Guys following suit in January 1972. No 258H is seen at Walsall bus station in June 1972 in company with similar 255H, which was outshopped from repaint minus its suffix.

Left: Walsall was not left without veteran vehicles. Dating from 1951, Park Royal-bodied Guy Arab III No 133L, with constant-mesh gearbox, became a tuition vehicle in November 1971, working on in this capacity for nearly two years. It is seen in Bridge Street, Walsall, in March 1973. Walsall originally had 50 buses with these bodies, half on Guy chassis and half on Leyland Titan PD2/1.

Left: Walsall also had 10 solidly built if rather wistful-looking Roe-bodied Leyland PD2/12 Titans. Three of these 1953 buses, 815/6/8L, were repainted into PTE livery and ran until 1973. No 816L, seen in March 1972 shortly after repaint, has just turned into Highfield Road, Burntwood.

Right: Arguably Walsall's most obscure routes were two Friday market-day services to Lichfield — the 45 from Beaudesert and the 46 from Goosemoor Green — which required the allocation of at least one short single-decker at Walsall. By the early 1970s the regular performer was 808L, a 1953 Leyland Royal Tiger with Park Royal body, although another (810L), refitted as a coach, was available. With destination incorrectly spelt, 808L is seen on 24 March 1972, at which time the pair had around another year to run. It was succeeded on these duties by other short single-deckers, such as ex-Birmingham Marshall-bodied Fleetlines, an ex-West Bromwich Leyland Tiger Cub and 707N, an ex-Wolverhampton AEC Reliance. WMPTE eventually had to make severe cuts to its services in Staffordshire, the 45 and 46 being withdrawn from 5 September 1976. Meanwhile 808L passed to Chase Terrace Comprehensive School and later into preservation, and now forms part of the collection at The Transport Museum, Wythall.

A RUN AROUND WALSALL BUS STATION

Walsall bus station was a hive of interest before the PTE took over and, with vehicles transfers and livery developments, continued to be the cause of reckless exposition of photographic film for several years thereafter. Nothing better sums up the approach adopted by Walsall's former General Manager, Ronald Edgley Cox, than buses 821-5. Five vehicles, all different, they were lightweights purchased for comparison trials, but none was adopted as the future standard. Nos 821-3 were exhibited at the 1954 Commercial Motor Show, and 824/5 at the next one, in 1956. Oh yes, there was a trolleybus at each Show too. Getting buses exhibited at the Show was an obsession, but did it improve the breed? Walsall's bus station was soon rebuilt, reopening on 31 August 1975 with completely revised loading arrangements.

Left: The maximum length for double-deckers was still 27ft when this Daimler CVG5 with Northern Counties body was built in 1954. Squeezing in 65 seats thus raised eyebrows at the time. No 821L is seen on 16 January 1971.

Right: An AEC Regent V with Park Royal body, 822L seated a more conservative 61. Also recorded on 16 January 1971, it would be withdrawn later that year without receiving PTE colours.

Left: No 822L was unlucky, for Mr Edgley Cox, now PTE Chief Engineer, generally seemed kindly disposed to buses from his Walsall fleet, even those that were highly non-standard. No 823L, a Leyland PD2 with semi-automatic gearbox and 61-seat Metro-Cammell body, still looks fresh in June 1972.

Right: The 1956 Show coincided with the relaxation in length to 30ft for double-deckers. Daimler CVG6-30 No 824, photographed on 19 October 1971, seated 74 in its Willowbrook body. Nos 821/3/4 all received PTE colours but were withdrawn in 1973.

Left: No 825L was a 1956 Crossley Bridgemaster with AEC running units and 72-seat Crossley body. Birmingham City Transport had had a similar bus, 3228, but BCT's engineers had managed to persuade the accountants that it would be more economic to let it go, cheering mightily when they finally agreed in 1969 — imagine their dismay to discover another when the PTE took over! No 825L remained on operational strength until 1971. *Chris Aston / Omnicolour*

Right: Walsall bought one Leyland Atlantean, delivered in 1959. Its Metro-Cammell body was 'semi-lowbridge', which meant a sunken gangway at the rear of the upper deck. Seen on 16 June 1972, 841L was converted to OMO in October of that year, lasting until 1977.

Left: Dennis Loline 800L, seen at Walsall bus station in August 1971, had been an exhibit at the 1958 Commercial Motor Show, and another 16 Lolines — 842-9 and 878-85 — were received by Walsall in 1960. All had Willowbrook bodies. The first few (800/42-8L) were overhauled and repainted into PTE livery upon Certificate of Fitness expiry at 12 years, but costs were high, and the remainder were withdrawn. All were out of use at Walsall by the end of 1973, but 842-5L were briefly returned to service at ex-Midland Red garages in 1974.

CERTIFICATES OF FITNESS

Every bus in passenger service in Britain had to have a current Certificate of Fitness. The initial CoF with which buses entered service lasted seven years (increased from five in 1956), following which operators overhauled and offered them for renewal, usually getting a five-year 'ticket'. After twelve years bus bodies could be getting tired, and some operators elected to sell their buses rather than overhaul them again at this age. BCT had continued major overhauls every five years, with intermediate attention. Its well-specified and well-maintained double-deckers were always overhauled again, easily gaining a third five years — and a fourth, if required. The longevity of the other municipalities' buses varied enormously: many of Wolverhampton's Strachans-bodied vehicles were not overhauled even at seven years, but some Coventry and West Bromwich Daimler CVG6/Metro-Cammell buses proved capable of 20. With increasing pay rates for workshop staff and a 50% grant for new buses, WMPTE gradually moved towards a 12-year life for its buses.

Left: There were five of these 1961 Daimler CVG6 buses, 886-90L, with 72-seat Metro-Cammell bodies. Most ran until 1977, outliving the contemporary ex-Walsall Regent Vs. The 241 was an off-peak variant of the Walsall–New Invention–Willenhall 41 service and ran via Wood Lane Estate, Short Heath, served at peak times by the 40; these services were eventually 'rationalised' as the 341, all journeys running via the estate. By 1973 the boys in the back room had issued a decree that entrance doors should be entirely blue. This made sense on folding doors, but presumably it never struck them that it would look ridiculous on sliders. No 886L makes the point at Wisemore on 29 March 1973.

Left: Walsall had 10 AEC Regent V buses dating from 1961, of which 891-5L, like the Daimlers, had Metro-Cammell bodies. No 893L is seen at Cannock bus station on the Lime Pit Lane circular, which took 24 minutes to operate in one direction and a further 24 in the other; running hourly in each direction, the service therefore required only one vehicle overall. It was, however, operated jointly with Midland Red, which numbered it 838/839; Midland Red was responsible on Sundays and at each end of the day from Monday to Friday and thus did not require an additional vehicle to run it, while Walsall Corporation and, later, WMPTE provided the service at peak times on weekdays and in its entirety on Saturdays, when Midland Red could be heavily involved with longer-distance services. *Paul Roberts*

Left: AEC Regent Vs 896-900L had Willowbrook bodywork. Along with the five Metro-Cammell-bodied Regents, 896/7L were overhauled and repainted in PTE livery upon expiry of their second, five-year CoF, generally continuing in service until 1975/6, but the cost of work on the Willowbrooks meant that 898-900L were not so blessed. No 900L, with Walsall's highest fleet number, is seen in August 1971.

Above: Fleetline/Metro-Cammell 3371 of 1964 passes Moseley Road garage on 2 March 1972. Routes 48 and 49 had passed from Moseley Road to Yardley Wood on 20 February, the 50 moving to Liverpool Street on 5 March, when Moseley Road garage closed. It had opened as a tramcar depot on New Year's Day 1907, converting to buses from 2 October 1949, and in December 1973 would be reopened as a short-term measure to house ex-Midland Red buses, finally closing again in November 1975 and thereafter becoming an engineering-training centre for WMPTE.

Below: Distinctive vehicles at Acocks Green garage for many years until their withdrawal in June 1972 were two experimental Gardner 5LW-powered lightweight buses — 3001, a 1952 Guy Arab with Saunders-Roe body, and 3002, a 1954 Daimler CLG5/Metro-Cammell. The latter is seen parked on the forecourt of Acocks Green garage prior to repainting (in the spring of 1970) in WMPTE livery.
Royston Morgan

Right: Guy 3001 in Colmore Row on 21 March 1972.

Above: Introduced in October 1972, WMPTE's Travelcard allowed unrestricted travel for four weeks on West Midlands bus services (except the premium-fare night services), initially for just £4; a boon to regular travellers and permitting the speedier loading of OMO vehicles, it proved an immediate success, and subsequent variants were valid on local trains. To supplement permanent sales outlets Tyburn Road Works converted redundant ex-BCT Guys 2555 and 2607 and Daimlers 2819/20 into sales vehicles, which for the first few weeks were parked at strategic points across the PTE's territory, while a further Guy, 2548, became a promotional vehicle (and is now preserved, restored as a BCT bus, at Aston Manor Transport Museum); all five were renumbered in the service-vehicle series. Here a queue lines up to buy Travelcards on 194 (formerly 2607) at the junction of Bull Street and Dale End, Birmingham, while 197 (ex 2548) pauses during its promotional duties. Between them is the doyen of the same batch, 2526, still hard at work from Washwood Heath garage. These Guys dated from 1950/1.

Left: Birmingham's Centrebus service was introduced on 2 October 1972 to provide links not offered by ordinary buses, notably through a recently pedestrianised area. Six small Commers had been ordered to fulfil this requirement but did not enter service until mid-November, pending which ex-BCT single-deck Marshall-bodied Daimler Fleetlines dating from 1965 trundled sedately around. No 3470 is on normal roads as it makes the tight turn from Dale End into Albert Street on 3 October. *E. V. Trigg / The Transport Museum, Wythall*

Left: The Centrebus Commers, 4236-41, were allocated to Miller Street garage and had bodies by Rootes of Maidstone, seating 18 or 19 and featuring doors on both sides, for use in the pedestrian areas. No 4240 shows this feature in Dale End in May 1973. Nos 4236-9 were 19-seaters, but 4240/1 seated 18 in a perimeter layout that allowed more standing passengers.

Right: Joining the Commers in the early days of the Centrebus service was CWO 516K, a demonstration Morrison Electricar battery-electric bus with obvious environmental benefits, especially in pedestrianised areas. Willowbrook built the 19-seat bodywork. Unfortunately it suffered the curse of battery-electrics, being unable to operate all day. It did not sound like a milk float, as might have been expected — more like a manic organ, the notes rising as more power was demanded. Here it hums through Victoria Square in November 1972.

Right: The battery-electric bus did not impress, but sadly its livery did. It was thought that the poor usage of Centrebus was due to a lack of impact among all the other buses and that orange would make the little vehicles stand out. Instead it made them look even more like vans, notably the Commers of Douglas, the contractor. No 4241 makes the point in Victoria Square in May 1973. The real problem was that the original route was too limited in scope, so from 14 January 1974 it was extended over a wider area; this proved so successful that it outgrew the Commers, and the Marshall-bodied Fleetlines took over again from 18 November 1974, Centrebus gaining service number 101 at the same time. Ironically it was on this service that the single-deck Fleetlines found their best role.

WTL

Centrebus

101

STARTING MONDAY 18 NOVEMBER 1974 LARGER CREAM-PAINTED SINGLE DECK BUSES WILL BE USED ON THE CENTREBUS SERVICE AND THESE WILL SHOW THE ROUTE NUMBER 101 AND SPECIAL ROUTE BOARDS.

STOP No. 10 AT BASKERVILLE HOUSE WILL BE WITHDRAWN FROM THE SAME DATE AND INTENDING PASSENGERS SHOULD USE PARADISE STREET OR PARADISE CIRCUS BUS STATION AS ALTERNATIVES.

F. G. SIMONS
Operations Manager
South Division

Enquiry Office
Great Charles Street
Birmingham B3 3HL
Telephone: 021-235 3542

Right: The PTE frustrated MCW by not favouring it with orders for Metro-Scanias. Only one such vehicle was delivered, No 4242 being placed in service in January 1973. It was a 47-seat BR111MH model. A minor livery modification from the summer of 1972 entailed the addition of WM logos on the front of new and repainted rear-engined buses, while the green disc seen here in the windscreen identified a vehicle fitted with a two-way radio connected to a control room, this system having been introduced in June 1972. When photographed in 1979 No 4242 was working from Selly Oak garage on service 54; this was introduced experimentally in November 1978, serving Birmingham's huge Queen Elizabeth Hospital and linking it with the 11 (Outer Circle) and the 21 (City–Bangham Pit), and continued until the 21 itself was re-routed in August 1980 to serve the hospital. No 4242 would be withdrawn the same year and sold in January 1981. *Royston Morgan*

Above: While many relatively modern but poorly designed buses would have short lives, the old BCT 'Standards' could go on and on. Insufficient deliveries of new vehicles and shortages of spare parts due to national industrial unrest meant that many of the old-timers had to be recertified upon expiry of their Certificates of Fitness. To assist, short-term recertifications began at the end of 1972, the buses in question being prepared at garages instead of Tyburn Road Works. This usually got them another couple of years' life, but as a result of this work some venerable 25xx Guys gained a CoF longer than had been granted at their previous full BCT overhaul at Tyburn Road — which suggests either that the previous examiner was unduly cautious or that lower standards were now acceptable to the Ministry! The most obvious indication externally of a garage recertification was the replacement of BCT blue by the WMPTE shade, the cream being left untouched, although the garage dealing with Guy 3028 got the message wrong and reapplied BCT blue. This bus then became one of five repainted early in 1973 at Walsall, losing the khaki roof but retaining the thin blue line under the lower-saloon windows, in which condition it is seen entering Colmore Row on 14 June. Somebody must then have supplied Walsall Works with a can of khaki paint, because another five 'Standards' repainted there subsequently (among them 2564, seen on page 1) re emerged with khaki roofs.

Left: Lower Bull Street on 15 May 1973, and Perry Barr's 3131 has cream fleet numbers, having been repainted at West Bromwich. Black fleet numbers in the orthodox position were soon applied in lieu. No 2600 would be similarly treated later in the year.

Left: At last a promotion structure for conductresses was put in place, when, following agreement with the trade union, women drivers were permitted from 1 April 1973. Every bus that could be adapted for one-*person* operation was now considered for conversion, and Birmingham's Leyland Atlanteans, 3230-40, were rebuilt in early 1973, the work including relocation of the service-number box, previously operated from the upper saloon. No 3230, had begun life in 1960 as a Leyland demonstrator (hence its Lancashire registration, 460 MTE) but was built with BCT in mind, and its success prompted the purchase of the other 10, delivered in 1961, for evaluation alongside 10 Daimler Fleetlines, 3241-50. All had Metro-Cammell bodies. It was the only one delivered with Leyland's Atlantean badge on the front, still in place on 15 June 1973 as the bus tackles the brief climb away from Camp Hill in Bradford Street before making the long descent to Birmingham's Markets Quarter.

Below: The extent of the rebuilding undertaken as part of OPO conversion is apparent from this view of Atlantean 3236, still in BCT livery but with PTE fleetnames, in August 1970. The bus is seen in Highfield Road, Hall Green, completing a cross-city journey on the 29 from Kingstanding Circle; the conductor has already wound up the 30 destinations for the northbound trip. The 29/30 in this form would disappear on 28 February 1971, when South Division introduced major service changes.

Right: Birmingham's first batch of Fleetlines, 3241-50, delivered in 1962, proved unsuitable for OPO conversion, repositioning of the route numbers being even more problematic than on the Atlanteans, which had more space between the top of the windscreens and the upper-saloon floor. Another bus that was not converted was Walsall's first Fleetline, 1L, its short length with no front overhang meaning that the entrance door was not alongside the driver. An exhibit at the 1962 Commercial Motor Show, it had 64-seat Northern Counties bodywork and was one of the first to receive cream-roof livery, in December 1971. Seen at Colmore Circus, Birmingham, on 14 June 1973, it would be taken out of service the following year.

Below: The extra length of Walsall's later Fleetlines was sufficient to allow an additional, narrow entrance door ahead of the front axle, provided on Northern Counties bodies built from 1965 to squarer proportions. On 2 August 1973 No 50L stands alongside an early example of 200 new double-deckers on Bristol VRT chassis, ordered due to an inadequate supply of Daimler Fleetlines. The bodies were constructed by Metro-Cammell. The first, 4343, was exhibited at the 1972 Commercial Motor Show (Edgley Cox still getting a vehicle exhibited there!), entering service in November, but bulk deliveries did not begin until the spring of 1973. The VRTs only ever ran from Walsall and the Wolverhampton garages. The arrival of all 200 in the two towns was a significant modernisation, of which the South Division, with its still-large fleet of 1950-4 Birmingham 'Standards', was a little envious. By contrast, withdrawals of Bristol VRTs began as early as 1980: a financial crisis meant serious service cuts, so the PTE stored and sold 4374-4442 upon expiry of their first Certificate of Fitness rather than pay the labour costs of overhauling them. *E. V. Trigg / The Transport Museum, Wythall*

Above: The Northern Counties bodies on Walsall's 1963/4 Fleetlines were slightly longer than that on the first and permitted 70 seats. No 9L loads at Blakenall in August 1971. Note that its repaint has left unscathed Walsall's classic striped used-ticket bin.

Above: Two of Walsall's 1963/4 Fleetlines, 17 and 24, received post-1965-style front ends in the Corporation era, and in 1971/2 the remainder were given additional front doors to permit their use on OPO services. The work was carried out by Lex Garages, which replaced the lower-deck wrap-around windscreens with flat glasses and then had to match these with the rounded profile of the upper deck. The result, by common consent, looked most awkward, but in rebuilt form these buses proved useful workhorses, most serving until 1976/7. No 19L was one of several transferred to Wolverhampton, where passengers are seen being subjected to an extremely spirited turn into Exchange Street in March 1973.

Below: The last of Walsall's 1964 Fleetlines, 30L (which actually entered service in January 1965), was built with a flat front and looked more like a typical Northern Counties product, and the addition of the front door was much simpler on this bus. It is pictured loading at Walsall bus station in November 1972.

Right: Delicensed in 1973 was the last of Wolverhampton's two Guy Wulfrunians. The Wulfrunian combined the modern idea of entrance ahead of the front axle with a front engine, but unfortunately this latter was the large and heavy Gardner 6LX, which put platform space at a premium and created problems with front axle loadings. Both Wolverhampton examples had East Lancs bodies, but, whereas 70N was to the usual Wulfrunian configuration, 71N of 1962 attempted to solve some of the weight-distribution problems with a shorter front overhang. As a result it had its entrance behind the front axle, thus giving little obvious advantage over the Arab but retaining several other engineering nightmares. Withdrawn in May 1973, it is pictured on 25 July at Wolverhampton's Oxford Street yard in company with Arab 215N, doubly doomed by dint of Strachans bodywork and fire damage. *E. V. Trigg / The Transport Museumn, Wythall*

Right: A further bus to be found delicensed in Wolverhampton's Oxford Street yard after withdrawal in May 1973 was 252H, a 1953 Guy with ECW 26-seat body, one of two purchased by West Bromwich Corporation from London Transport in 1961.

Right: Wolverhampton had a small assortment of full-size single-deckers, all allocated to its Bilston Street garage. One of three AEC Reliances, with dual-door 40-seat Park Royal bodies, that had been used introduced one-man operation in 1963, No 705N is seen in West Castle Street, Bridgnorth, on 12 May 1973. The principal service between Wolverhampton and Bridgnorth was the 17, the 31 being a less-frequent link via Pattingham and Ackleton. The Bridgnorth services would be handed over to Midland Red in December 1973.

Left: The Bridgnorth services were among those terminating at Railway Drive, Wolverhampton — the 'country' bus station — from where AEC Swift 712N is seen departing on service 17 on 22 March 1973. Six of these Strachans-bodied Swifts had been bought by Wolverhampton in 1967. Despite their dual-doors layout they seated 54, this being achieved by 3+2 seating at the rear. Two were sold to Northampton Corporation in April 1972, and none would wear PTE colours, the batch being eliminated in 1974. The inability to match the green paint after minor accident damage or panel changes was classic Wolverhampton!
E. V. Trigg / The Transport Museum, Wythall

Left: The 1967 Swifts were accompanied by six Strachans-bodied Daimler Roadliners. These too had short lives, but some did gain PTE livery. Roadliner 716N is seen in August 1973.

Left: Although having a higher fleet number than the Swifts and Roadliners 720N actually preceded them, entering service in October 1966. Also Strachans-bodied, the chassis was a somewhat less sophisticated Ford R226. Seen in Queen Square, Wolverhampton, on 23 August 1973, it was destined to outlive the Swifts and the Roadliners, being transferred in October 1975 to Perry Barr (as 1720) for further service alongside the ex-BCT Fords and ultimately becoming a tuition vehicle before final withdrawal in April 1977.

Left: The December 1973 takeover of Midland Red's local services in the West Midlands meant that integration of operators' services could begin in earnest. Some 413 buses, 170 services, eight garages (and one parking area) plus all the staff to run them transferred on 3 December 1973, Moseley Road garage being reopened to operate services run hitherto from Digbeth garage, retained by Midland Red. At the same time 16 Wolverhampton-area services passed from the PTE to Midland Red, but the Cannock services operated from Walsall remained with the PTE, at least for the time being. Midland Red had built its own buses for nearly half a century, and 90 of its D9 class passed to the PTE, among them Moseley Road's 4866, seen at Solihull station on 28 August 1974. To reduce the immediate impact on the works capacity of both organisations it was agreed that for the time being ex-Midland Red buses would continue to be repainted at their former operator's Central Works in Carlyle Road, Birmingham. However, the colour and location of the fleet numbers, in cream below rather than black above the windows, on 4866 implies a PTE repaint, probably at Walsall. Poignantly, the crew are still in full Midland Red uniform.

Left: Midland Red's first rear-engined double-deckers were 50 Daimler Fleetlines with Alexander bodywork, which were delivered in 1963 and formed the company's DD11 (later D11) class. Of these 21 passed to the PTE, among them Hartshill's 5255, seen approaching Stourbridge garage, terminus of route 245, on 30 April 1974.

> **MIDLAND RED**
> Associated with the National Bus Company
>
> **WM**
> **WEST MIDLANDS**
>
> **TRANSFER**
> OF
> **SERVICES**
> FROM
> **MIDLAND RED**
> TO
> **WEST MIDLANDS P.T.E.**
>
> FROM MONDAY 3rd DECEMBER, 1973, MOST MIDLAND RED BUS SERVICES IN THE BLACK COUNTRY, SUTTON COLDFIELD, CHELMSLEY WOOD AND SOLIHULL AREAS WILL BE TRANSFERRED TO WEST MIDLANDS P.T.E.
>
> GENERALLY, ROUTE NUMBERS, TIMETABLES AND SINGLE FARES WILL NOT BE ALTERED ON THIS DATE. WHEN CHANGES ARE MADE DETAILS WILL BE PUBLICISED. FOR FULL DETAILS SEE PRESS PUBLICITY OR PHONE ANY W.M.P.T.E. OR MIDLAND RED OFFICE.

Left: The ex-Midland Red operations were run as one unit until shared between the North and South divisions. Among additions to the South Division was Sutton Coldfield garage, where BMMO S16 No 5116 is seen displaying a nostalgic 'destination' on 4 April 1974. The PTE inherited 14 S16s, which had constant-mesh gearboxes (the bulk of the ex-Midland Red stock being semi-automatic) and were not fitted for OPO; only one (5105) received PTE colours, and that was as a training bus. *E. V. Trigg / The Transport Museum, Wythall*

Left: Nineteen Leyland PSU3 Leopards of Midland Red's 1962/3 LS18 class came to the PTE. Most were bodied by Willowbrook, including 5195 of Moseley Road, here on ex-Digbeth work. The location is Hobs Moat Road, just inside Solihull, the date 31 May 1975. These Leopards were long-lived for non-standard vehicles, many running until 1978, and Weymann-bodied 5161 became a mobile uniform store in 1980.

Below left : An arguably surprising route to pass to the PTE was the 250, which crossed the county boundary to Kinver, in Staffordshire. Weymann-bodied Leopard 5148 makes its way through the construction works for Stourbridge ring road on 30 April 1974. Stourbridge merited early research because of the costs of the Stourbridge Town–Stourbridge Junction rail service, although this survived the PTE's first major area market-research study, which produced a revised service network from 5 December 1976. Stourbridge was linked to Birmingham by both local rail and the 130 bus service, but both survived, as they were not considered to compete with each other.

Left: The great bus famine of the mid-1970s had its origins in the run-down condition of many of the ex-Midland Red vehicles and the failure of the supply industry, riven by disputes, to provide vital spares. Ex-Birmingham 1965 Fleetline/Park Royal 3520 was loaned by Miller Street to Stourbridge, which, unlike most ex-Midland Red garages, bothered to fit a destination blind, even though this one is adrift! The bus is seen loading at a temporary stop (still with Midland Red lettering) in Worcester Street, Stourbridge, while working the S46 service on 14 May 1974. Stourbridge's S-prefix locals disappeared in the major revision of the town's services on 5 December 1976, the new arrangements having numbers in the high 2xx series.

Left: With the 413 Midland Red buses came some service vehicles, of which arguably the most interesting were two former BMMO D7 double-deckers. Originally bus 4392, WMPTE 218 still wore its former owner's livery for towing vehicles when photographed at Dudley bus station on 30 April 1974.

Right: Of Birmingham's 1964 batch of 50 Metro-Cammell bodied Fleetlines 3391-3400 introduced modernised front ends with two experimental designs of windscreen. The 'V' screen, with cheaper, flat glass, was adopted as standard, and 3396-8 and 3400 would remain the only ones with curved screens. No 3397 was on loan to Hartshill garage when photographed at Dudley on 30 April 1974, all too typically working without a destination blind.

Right: Ex-Birmingham Daimler CVG6s were also loaned to Midland Red garages, reintroducing open rear platforms after many years. They must have seemed archaic. Loaned to Hartshill and embarking on a rare rural treat, 22-year old 2784 climbs Castle Hill, Dudley, on 30 April 1974. The 259 was an infrequent service to Swindon — to the west of Wallheath, not in Wiltshire.

Below right: In 1968 had come Edgley Cox's final opportunity to exhibit a bus bearing the Walsall Corporation name at the Commercial Motor Show, and he took it with this giant 36ft-long showstopper. The Daimler chassis was not a Fleetline but a prototype for a South African contract, its Cummins V6-200 engine being mounted in the rear offside corner, allowing the additional exit to be at the extreme rear. Despite having two doors the Northern Counties body seated 86 (later reduced to 85). Finished in a unique livery of pale blue and ivory, it was intended as a one-man-operated vehicle, with a closed-circuit camera covering the rear exit and relaying a picture to a monitor located just behind the front door. However, in 1968 CCTV technology was not up to the rigours of on-road use, and the bus had to be worked with a conductor, usually on the 118 Walsall–Birmingham service. Pictured still in its original colour scheme, 56L received PTE livery in the autumn of 1973 and between January 1974 and its withdrawal later that year spent a brief period working from the ex-Midland Red garage at Hartshill, where the staff were proud to demonstrate their willingness and ability to drive anything, in contrast to their union colleagues down the road! *Stephen Davies / The Transport Museum, Wythall*

Below: Not every veteran in Dudley bus station in 1974 was working from an ex-Midland Red garage. Recorded on 30 April on a short working of the 74, 17 year-old ex-West Bromwich Daimler CVG6/Willowbrook 193H was still based at its home town's Oak Lane garage.

Above: All buses suitable for one-person operation had been so adapted by January 1974. The South Division decided that its last route to be converted to OPO should be the Outer Circle, which had been Fleetline-operated for some years, so on 17 February 1974 it reverted temporarily to BCT 'Standards', enabling other routes to be converted first, and South Division OPO to reach 82%. Prior to this there had been attempts to persuade Birmingham trade-union representatives to accept ex-Wolverhampton 72-seat Guy Arabs. However, they preferred their old open-platform buses, so 1962 Arab IV/Metro-Cammell 69N, pictured in Exchange Street, Wolverhampton, in August 1973, remained in its home town.

Below: Of the ex-Wolverhampton Guy Arab V buses 41 were bodied by Strachans, 10 dating from 1965, the remainder 1967. The first eight were overhauled, at considerable expense, but the deterioration of the bodywork was so great that the rest began to be parked up as early as 1972. The failure of the plan to transfer Wolverhampton Arabs to Birmingham was probably the last straw, and WMPTE gave up on the Strachans bodies, formally withdrawing the unoverhauled examples. No 208N, a Cleveland Road-allocated bus seen in Queen Square, Wolverhampton, in August 1973, was one of very few of the 1967 batch to receive PTE colours. The chassis of some of the Guys, including this one, were sold to Hong Kong to be rebodied, but this was not an economic proposition in the UK at a time when the purchase of new rear-engined buses suitable for OPO was encouraged by Government grants.

RENUMBERING OF BUS SERVICES

To avoid duplication of service numbers and to obtain a logical system during area network revisions a numbering scheme for PTE services was developed:

1-99	Birmingham city services (basically ex-Birmingham City Transport)
100-99	Services from Birmingham to points outside the city, plus Sutton and Solihull locals (basically ex Midland Red)
200-99	Dudley services (basically ex Midland Red)
300-99	Walsall services, including Staffordshire
400-99	Sandwell services (ex West Bromwich and Midland Red)
500-99	Wolverhampton services
600-99	North Division works services
700-99	North Division schools services
800-51	South Division works services
852-99	South Division schools services
900-99	Limited-stop, hospital, football, dog-track, supermarket-contract and bingo services

Most Birmingham-area services could retain their existing numbers. In practice the South Division works and schools services became intermixed.

Of the services taken over from Midland Red, some in the Wolverhampton area had been in that company's 8xx series but had been renumbered upon takeover, while the D- and S-prefixed locals in Dudley, Stourbridge, Sutton and Solihull were swallowed up in area network revisions or renumbered when opportune.

The ex-Walsall, West Bromwich and Wolverhampton services were frequently the old Corporation numbers with the appropriate hundred figure added, although service revisions overtook some traditional routes before renumbering. Some Walsall services were renumbered twice, a start having been made in the early days of the PTE to place them in the 2xx series later required for ex-Midland Red services.

It was decided that the Coventry services were so removed from the rest of the system that they could keep their existing numbers. Suffix letters were for short workings, however, so use of these for groupings of similar services was frowned upon; for example, Coventry routes 9/9A became 29 and 39.

Above: West Bromwich had a number of low-height Fleetlines, and they were given this special livery. Fourteen were built in 1967 with MCW bodies. They were delivered with 'V'-windscreens, but, unlike the ex-Birmingham examples, most were modified to this style. Seen in Anchor Road, Aldridge, in April 1974, No 109H was an interesting participant on the Walsall–Sutton Coldfield service, with its short workings between Walsall and Aldridge.

Below: Formerly operated jointly by Walsall and West Bromwich, the basically hourly 53 service from West Bromwich to Aldridge, with occasional extensions to Streetly, became 353 in the Walsall series. However, although Walsall participated in its operation the route did not actually serve the town, and it was further renumbered, as 453, in July 1977. This rare shot at Aldridge features two ECW-bodied Daimler Fleetlines of different operators. WMPTE 117H was one of seven delivered in 1969 to West Bromwich Corporation, while Harper Bros 33 was one of a pair new in April 1973 with Leyland 680 engines instead of the more usual Gardner units. Midland Red would buy out Harper Bros in 1974, using proceeds from the sale to the PTE of its own services in Birmingham and the Black Country. *Paul Roberts*

Above: As a result of local-government reorganisation Coventry's municipal buses were added to the PTE area with effect from 1 April 1974. The Midland Red and Coventry takeovers increased the WMPTE fleet by more than 50%, and it now stood at around 2,600 buses. Coventry had ceased repainting buses in its own colours before the takeover, hence at Pool Meadow on 22 February 1974 the future 292Y already wears WMPTE blue and cream but with Coventry fleetnames. Most of the Coventry fleet was built in the city by Daimler. CVG6 buses with Metro-Cammell 'Orion' bodies were standard for many years and still made up around a third of the fleet upon the handover to WMPTE. This example dated from 1961.

Below: When Coventry ordered its first 22 rear-engined double-deckers for 1964 delivery it caused real controversy by opting for Leyland Atlanteans rather than locally built Daimler Fleetlines, and the transgression was not repeated. The body contract raised eyebrows too, being placed with Willowbrook after many years of Metro-Cammell patronage. No 344Y unusually sports an ivory roof at Pool Meadow on 6 May 1975.

Above: Coventry had two garages, Harnall Lane and Sandy Lane, the allocation of each bus being denoted by the 'H' or 'S' above the windscreen. In the final years of the Coventry undertaking its livery of maroon and ivory was simplified to the layout seen on 12Y in Trinity Street on 18 May 1978. The bodies of the 1-22 batch were built by East Lancs or its subsidiary, Neepsend, this bus being an East Lancs example. 'Monobus' was Coventry's description of an OMO vehicle.

Below: By 1974 Coventry's six ECW-bodied Bristol RESL6G single-deckers of 1967 were becoming due for CoF renewal and thus a major overhaul. Without a need for all six, Coventry advertised four for sale shortly before the takeover, but WMPTE, hard-pressed for single-deckers following the Midland Red acquisition, managed to halt their disposal, and on 1 April 1974 Nos 517/8/20/1 moved to Wolverhampton as 4443-6; Nos 516/9, with 'Y' suffix added, initially remained at Coventry. No 519Y followed the others in June, but by this time there was already a 4447 in service, so at Wolverhampton it reverted to plain 519. Having tied itself in a knot with these fleet numbers, the PTE eventually renumbered the entire batch as 5516-21 in September 1976. Photographed at Bilston bus station on 4 June 1975, No 4444 was working route 63 (Sedgley–Bilston–Rocket Pool), formerly Midland Red's 863 and destined, in modified form, to become the 563 under the renumbering of Wolverhampton-area services; behind is ex-BCT Guy 2957, on loan to Wolverhampton and covering the ex-Corporation 45 service.

Right: ECW bodywork was also to be found on 18 Coventry Daimler Fleetlines, 23-40, delivered in 1968. Coventry may have adopted PTE colours before takeover but seemed to want to make a point, 28Y being outshopped in PTE blue and Coventry ivory — a livery it still carried when seen at Pool Meadow in March 1978. Built with centre exit doors, these buses had by the time of the PTE takeover already been converted to single-door by Coventry's excellent body shop at Sandy Lane garage.

Above: Representing the exact opposite to 28Y in the previous picture, 31Y was repainted in Coventry red with WMPTE cream. This scene, at Broadgate, dates from 22 February 1974, hence the retention of the Coventry fleetname and coat-of-arms.

Left: The 1969 batch of 18 Fleetlines, 41-58, had dual-door East Lancs bodies and were rebuilt to single-door in 1974/5. One of the last to wear Coventry's pre-1970 livery for rear-engined buses, 57 had already received its 'Y' suffix by 22 February 1974, when this photograph was taken at Pool Meadow.

Left: Seen at Broadgate on the same day is the future 65Y, bearing Coventry fleetnames and coat-of-arms on WMPTE livery. This belonged to the 1970 batch of 18 Fleetlines (59-76), all originally with dual-door bodywork by Park Royal, although in 1972 the last of the batch had received a new East Lancs body as a result of serious fire damage.

Above: The Park Royal-bodied buses, 59-75Y, did not lend themselves to single-door conversion, and only one (70Y) was dealt with. Instead Coventry's Sandy Lane body shop performed similar conversions on many of the ex-Midland Red DD13-class Alexander-bodied Fleetlines. Demonstrating the quality of the work, 6283 is seen at The Parade, Sutton Coldfield, on 23 September 1978.

Right: A further 18 dual-door East Lancs-bodied Fleetlines, 77-94, were received in 1971, being converted to single door in the period 1977-9. Photographed before being rebuilt, 93Y leaves Pool Meadow on 18 March 1978.

Right: Coventry's final 48 Fleetlines, 95-142, delivered in 1972/3, had single-door East Lancs bodies, and the 1973 buses featured a simplified livery. In 1975 the 159 (Coventry–Birmingham) was still worked by ex-Midland Red buses running from the reopened Moseley Road garage in Birmingham, but recorded at Wells Green, Sheldon, on 19 May was 139Y, provided as a replacement for a vehicle failed at the Coventry end. You have to admire the driver's attempt at a destination — correct in both directions!

Left: A further Coventry order for East Lancs-bodied Fleetlines was delivered in the summer of 1974 and numbered 4447-66. The reason for 4465's appearance at Pool Meadow, Coventry, on the 159 on Monday 6 April 1981 (fortunately Birmingham was by now on the Coventry blind) was quite different from that pertaining to 139Y. Desperate to retain control of West Midlands County Council and aware that bus patronage was (very slightly) down on Mondays, the Conservatives thought it would be a good idea to fill the buses by introducing a 'Monday Funday' flat fare of 10p for adults and 5p for children, commencing 2 March 1981 and continuing for nine weeks (*i.e.* until the election); as a result every bus and driver available had to be put to work on longer routes like the 159, swamped by passengers travelling at a fraction of the normal 90p fare. The Conservatives then promised to continue the experiment beyond the election — which they lost — and by the time the incoming Labour administration halted the Monday Fundays (the last being 8 June) the scheme was estimated to have cost £1.5 million in lost income from Travelcards and other fares, as well as additional operating costs. Labour supporters should not feel too smug — Labour did away with the writer's beloved Birmingham City Transport and is thus forever cursed.

Right: By the time of the Coventry takeover WMPTE was suffering from the deteriorating condition of some of its other acquired buses, and industrial unrest around the country meant that deliveries of replacements were running late. Even Birmingham's trusty 'Standards' were getting rather too long in the tooth: ex-BCT AEC Matador 14 recovers Daimler CVG6 3214 at Bournville on 18 July 1974. *The Transport Museum, Wythall*

Above: Fortunately help was on the way. Coventry's buses were in excellent condition, and around 20 CVG6 models dating from 1957/8, rendered surplus by the arrival of 4447-66, were transferred to Birmingham's Acocks Green garage, primarily for the Outer Circle. The timing point in Cole Bank Road, Hall Green, accommodates two of them followed by an ex-Birmingham bus in WMPTE colours. No 211Y, new in January 1957, was the last of its batch to remain in service and one of very few still in Coventry's pre-1970 livery; 226Y, like the rest of the buses transferred, dated from 1958. South Division clerical staff often misread the 'Y' letter suffix as a '7', these two sometimes being recorded as 2117 and 2267; as a result the 'Y' was deleted and 1,000 added, so by the time of this photograph, taken on 11 October 1974, these buses had become 1211 and 1226.

Right: Acocks Green's ex-Coventry Daimlers could be seen on other services, but the chance of capturing two passing each other on anything but the Outer Circle was very low. No 1224 is seen in Bradford Street on 19 May 1975. This particular working did not run around the city-centre loop, instead commencing its next 32 journey, at the very height of the peak, from Ethel Street; such 'short' workings not only provided valuable space for passengers boarding after the city centre but could also save a complete bus in the timetable. Heading in the opposite direction is 1250, its vinyl fleetname peeling to reveal part of 'Coventry transport'. Repaints of transferred CVG6s into PTE colours began in January 1975: Coventry CVG6s repainted at home gained all-blue bulkheads (see 292Y on page 42), but these would receive the usual cream upper works.

Right: BMMO S23s lasted in quantity at Stourbridge garage, firstly because a serious accident involving a Leyland National initially discouraged drivers there and secondly because two services passed beneath a railway bridge in Station Road, Old Hill, which was too low for the Nationals' heating pod. To permit the type's use the road was closed and lowered during early 1978 — shortly before Leyland introduced the 'podless' National! Here 5929, a Stourbridge-based S23 with an S17 grille, loads at Halesowen bus station on 11 October 1977. The last BMMO buses, S23s 5932/81, would survive — at Stourbridge garage — until January 1981.

Left: With the Midland Red transfer came 33 Leyland Nationals, and this type of bus became the WMPTE standard single-decker too — not that there was a lot of choice in the market place if you wanted a single-decker with a low-step entrance. Two orders, each for 30, were delivered between August and December 1974 as a single batch numbered 4467-4526. To get them into service quickly 10 were used first as 52-seaters in all-over cream, seating capacity being reduced to the preferred 50 (with luggage pens) and blue added as soon as possible. Stourbridge's 4516 is able to pass beneath the railway bridge at Old Hill without risk of losing its pod while working the 202 service in January 1979, a month troubled by an exceptional amount of snow.
Brian Tromans / The Transport Museum, Wythall

Right: Prototype Volvo Ailsas 4527-9 entered service towards the end of 1974. These were very different from the ubiquitous Fleetlines, having front engines, but unlike the disastrous Guy Wulfrunians they featured Volvo units which were compact yet still tough enough for the job. Alexander built the 79-seat bodywork. Having started life at Perry Barr the trio soon settled at Sutton Coldfield garage. No 4527 is seen bathed in sunshine in Navigation Street, Birmingham, on 18 June 1979.

Above: "There's a Tiger Cub on the 118!" was a cry that brought alarming visions of wildlife running amok; in reality it was the Leyland version that was on the loose on the Walsall–Birmingham service. Four 7ft 6in-wide Roe-bodied examples were purchased by West Bromwich Corporation, the first pair being received in 1960, the other in 1963.

No 250H was one of the latter and was Walsall's short-length single-decker for the Friday Lichfield market-day services 45/46 when it was awoken from its slumbers to assist the 118 on Tuesday 5 November 1974. It is seen leaving Birmingham's Bull Ring bus station.

Left: Around 1975 a concerted effort to expunge the colours of operators absorbed in 1969 overtook a notable cluster of survivors at Wolverhampton. Guy Arab IV/ Metro-Cammell 6N of 1957, which had already outlasted its 17 brothers by around two years when it succumbed to PTE livery in February, is seen in Princess Street in June. Meanwhile, at Coventry, where short-term recertification was needed for its oldest CVG6s, the Harnall Lane paint shop quietly repainted these vehicles in their original colours of maroon and ivory, allegedly to minimise undercoating and to use up paint stocks. Senior management remained blissfully unaware of this occurrence so far east of the PTE's Birmingham head office, by now relocated to Summer Lane.

Above: A route between Wolverhampton and Sedgley along Northway, to serve a new housing estate, was introduced on 5 October 1970. The 30ft-long Guy Arab IVs and nearly all the Arab Vs were blessed only with 8.4-litre Gardner 6LW engines, despite their size and 72-seat capacity, while the semi-automatic gearboxes also cost a little in performance. The Guys sounded powerful but, sadly, were not: the residents around Northway — and, no doubt, the bus drivers who rapidly changed down through the gears from fourth to first — were dismayed to find the Arabs struggled to climb this short but sharp hill. On wet days it was frequently necessary to ask a proportion of the passengers to get off, a situation familiar in earlier days but unexpected in the 1970s. Fortunately the sun is out for Arab V No 141N, one of 25

Park Royal-bodied examples delivered in 1963/4, as it hits the gradient in August 1975, with green fields, over the county boundary in Staffordshire, stretching out behind.

Below: By June 1975 a considerable number of ex-Birmingham Guys dating from 1950-3, rendered surplus at Hockley by the conversion of service 90 to Fleetlines, were in use at Wolverhampton, covering for much newer Guys off the road there. No 2953 adds to the mix of vehicles to be seen in Dudley on 28 August 1975 as it returns along Wolverhampton Street to its temporary home. The 58 used to be operated by Wolverhampton's trolleybuses, having being the Corporation's last such route prior to its conversion to motor bus in March 1967.

Above: Crossley-bodied Daimler CVG6 2847, new in 1952, was something of a celebrity vehicle, having been fitted with doors and heaters in BCT days. Seen in June 1975 navigating St Chad's Circus, here host to some of the many 'Standards' still on the road, No 2847 was by now resident at Perry Barr, a garage not normally associated with the 15 route, hence the vague destination. From 3 August Birmingham's destination-display traditions would be overturned: city-bound buses would show 'CITY' or, if the route began beyond the city boundary (as many now did), 'BIRMINGHAM'. The different short-working letters went too, all such journeys now being suffixed 'E' (for Exception) — rather unhelpful when combined with 'SERVICE EXTRA'. From the same date the three circular services, 8 (Inner), 11 (Outer) and 19 (City), were suffixed according to direction — 'C' for clockwise and 'A' for anticlockwise.

Right: Gardner engines were standard for the Fleetline and VRT buses, but supply difficulties led to some Fleetlines' receiving Leyland 680 units. The first 50 were 4530-79, allocated to South Division garages with a Leyland history, Perry Barr and Yardley Wood. Nos 4580-4629 had the usual Gardners, and all 100, entering service in 1975, had 76-seat Park Royal bodywork. Delivered alongside were 4630-4729, the second batch of 100 Bristol VRTs with MCW bodies. All the lower-deck windows on the nearside now included an opening vent, in an attempt to reduce summertime complaints. As with the earlier batch, some of the Bristol VRTs ran for only seven years, but 4682 was still working in July 1986 from Walsall, braving a windy day in Barr Common Road.

Top: Early in 1975 Willowbrook-bodied Daimler Fleetlines 360-4Y of 1965, already repainted in blue and cream and renumbered 1360-4, were transferred from Coventry to Dudley. No 1364 works the D3 from Dudley bus station on 28 August 1975.

Above: Surplus in their native city during the school holidays, more Coventry buses to be seen in Dudley during the summer of 1975 were VWK-registered CVG6s working from Hartshill garage, principally on the 245/6 'D&S' (local shorthand for Dudley and Stourbridge) services. No 239Y was recorded on 28 August 1975.

Above: High wage costs and slow deliveries led to a search in 1975 for second-hand rear-engined buses to accelerate the spread of OPO. However, everybody had the same idea, and good-quality buses were hard to find, the only fruits of the exercise being 14 1960 Leyland Atlanteans acquired from Kingston-upon-Hull Corporation. Among these were five (1142-6) with Metro-Cammell bodywork, of which 1142 (6342 KH), seen at Dudley shortly after purchase, retained its side destination box, albeit overpainted. Daimler CVG6

No 3119 alongside, on temporary loan, was working the D1 service. In September Dudley's 'D'-prefixed locals would be renumbered into the high 2xx series.

Below: The other nine ex-Hull Atlanteans (1147-9/51-6) had Roe bodies. No 1153 (2353 AT) is seen in August 1975 working the D4 from Dudley, but the second-hand Roes would become more familiar at Wolverhampton.

Above: The BMMO S17s were workmanlike buses, the last surviving with WMPTE until 1977. Rounding the traffic island at the junction of Hobs Moat Road, Old Lode Lane and Lode Lane, No 5497 of Moseley Road garage heads through Solihull on Saturday 31 May 1975 on a positioning journey on service A88, which linked the Rover works with central Birmingham by way of Olton and Acocks Green. Midland Red had numbered this as the X88, 'X' being used not just for high-profile longer-distance stage-carriage routes but also numerous works, RAF, schools and hospital services, but latterly the company decided that this series should be reserved for limited-stop services, hence the renumbering as A88, 'A' being already used locally for Austin works services to and from Longbridge. However, the PTE wished to eradicate prefix letters, so in due course the service would be renumbered yet again, becoming the 850.

Below: Planning South Division's integration of BCT and Midland Red services took a couple of years. The 55 was extended to Kingshurst in August 1974, and the 92 to Monkspath in April 1975, but the big changes began on 16 November 1975. Moseley Road and Sheepcote Street garages closed, and ex-Midland Red Fleetline double-deckers and BMMO, Leyland Leopard and National single-deckers were reallocated to ex-BCT garages. On the same date train services on the Dorridge and Shirley lines were improved, and by March 1976 bus/rail interchanges had been provided at Dorridge, Olton, Shirley and Solihull stations. Crossing Saltley Viaduct on 8 July 1976, dual-purpose BMMO S22 No 5899 provides comfortable accommodation on the busy service from Lea Hall garage.

Right: The difficulty of attracting people in affluent areas to public transport led to the introduction on 15 December 1975 of a Dial-a-Bus service in Knowle and Dorridge, subsequently (in July 1977) extended into Solihull. High telephone ownership was vital, as, unless pre-booked every day, passengers contacted a control room. They would then be collected as close as possible to their homes and delivered to another point on the Dial-a-Bus network, often Dorridge railway station for a fast trip by rail to central Birmingham — all by Travelcard, of course! Eight Ford A-series buses with Alexander (Belfast) 23-seat bodywork, small enough to penetrate the local estate roads, were introduced, numbered 4730-7 and operated from Acocks Green garage. These should have been sufficient, but their reliability record was so poor that former Centrebus Commers 4238/41 were brought in to assist. The Commers' offside doors had been removed and, thankfully, they had been repainted from orange back into blue and cream. The Transport & Road Research Laboratory assisted the experiment, but the labour-intensive control room added to the costs. In September 1978 the area reverted to traditional operation, the Ford As remaining for a while longer as ordinary fixed-route buses over the estate roads until drastic service cuts spelled their demise in November 1980. No 4734 is seen at Dorridge station on 1 August 1980.

Right: The Fords had been ordered following a trial of this Aberdeen vehicle on the Centrebus service. GSA 860N is seen at Miller Street garage on 19 June 1975.
The Transport Museum, Wythall

Below: Following the three prototype Volvo Ailsas a batch of 50 production buses, 4738-87, was delivered between January and May 1976 and allocated to the ex-Midland Red garages at Oldbury and Sutton Coldfield. Bodywork was again by Alexander. Oldbury's 4758 enjoys the spring sunshine at Bearwood bus station in May 1978 while on a service that used to be operated jointly by Midland Red and West Bromwich Corporation. *E. V. Trigg / The Transport Museum, Wythall*

Right: Leyland Nationals 4788-99 were intended primarily for contracted internal car-park shuttles and inter-suburban stage-carriage services for staff and local visitors to the National Exhibition Centre, opened in early 1976. Finished in the NEC house colours, they had two doors, to aid rapid loading and alighting. The stage-carriage services, introduced in January 1976, were the 197 to Solihull and 199 to Castle Vale, where 4791 is seen on 25 March 1976; from November the two services would be combined as the 199. When not required for shuttle duties the Nationals would appear on other single-deck routes. *E. V. Trigg / The Transport Museum, Wythall*

Left: One of the rare ex-BCT trolleybus routes, the 58 was operated by Coventry Road garage and in May 1976 was extended from the city boundary into Solihull to terminate at Birmingham International station, alongside the National Exhibition Centre. Ex-BCT Fleetline/Metro-Cammell 3543 of 1965 loads at Birmingham International on 21 October 1978. Rail was always a better option for the majority of travellers heading into the city centre, while the 159 Coventry–Birmingham service was quite able to deal with the lesser demand along the Coventry Road; extending the 58 was an early example (later repeated) of hope exceeding reality with regard to bus services and the nearby International Airport.

Right: Nowadays the entrance to the Airport is adjacent to Birmingham International Station, but the earlier entrance was much nearer the city boundary and justified running 'short' workings to it. Fleetline/Park Royal 3758 of 1968 sets down passengers at Wells Green, Sheldon, while working an Airport 'short' on 28 August 1979. This bus was one of several of its batch repainted at Walsall, hence the cream roof.

Above: Like many bus companies WMPTE became an 'accidental' operator of open-top buses after an unwise excursion by a driver under a low railway bridge. Dual-door Fleetline/Park Royal 3867 of 1969 was the victim and reappeared in October 1978 after conversion (by Moseley Road Training Centre) to open-top and single-entrance. It was used for special events such as this one on 14 April 1979, organised by BRMB Radio; making a surprise contribution to service 58, it is seen is on the old approach road to the airport. It would also be used for driving tuition, whatever the weather, as your author discovered on taking it out from undercover at Harborne garage on a perfectly dry day: the first brake application brought a reservoir of water to the front of the upper deck, soaking the driver through major leaks above his head.

Below: No 3867 formerly looked like this. No exciting events or excursions for No 3845, one of around 50 similar buses allocated for many years to Cotteridge garage and destined to plod up and down the Pershore Road; here it is pursued by later Fleetline/Park Royal 4275 as it wearily makes another circuit of Holloway Circus in May 1979. Nos 3781-3880, delivered in 1968/9, were the last buses to enter service with Birmingham City Transport. Their centre exit door was designed to speed unloading, but, as described on page 5, this was not to be.

Right: The reduction of conductor duties at West Bromwich meant that the town's Daimler CVG6/ Metro-Cammell buses were becoming increasingly surplus. In 1975 Nos 186H and 214-9H were loaned to Wolverhampton, while more joined those already at Walsall, but the OPO conversion from March 1976 of Walsall's Bloxwich group of one-time trolleybus services spelled the end of that haven also. Some moved to the South Division, arriving at Hockley in March and Liverpool Street in May, primarily for the cross-city service 15/16 (Hamstead–Yardley). Hockley's 235H, new in 1961, climbs Hob Moor Road on 24 August 1976. In December another one of the same batch, 237H, joined the ex-Midland Red garage at Sutton Coldfield.

Below: In November 1973 the PTE had tried to order another 600 Fleetlines, but Leyland would agree a contract for only 420 in addition to options for 80 secured by Coventry. The PTE's professional officers were less than pleased, and it was a particularly bad move on the part of British Leyland to upset the politicians on the WMPTA: Fleetline production had been transferred to Leyland, and the politicians became determined that the manufacture of complete buses would return to the West Midlands. Meanwhile the reduced order for 500 Fleetlines began to arrive at the beginning of 1976. The fleet numbers of new buses, having reached 4799, now leapfrogged those of the ex-Midland Red vehicles, recommencing at 6301. The original intention was that 6301-6570 should be bodied by MCW, 6571-6720 by Park Royal, and 6721-6800 by East Lancs; however, Coventry had ordered only 40 East Lancs bodies,

and Park Royal was very slow in supplying its contract, so 6691-6720 and 6761-6800 ended up being bodied by MCW. Again there was a shortage of Gardner engines, so 6301-6420 had Leyland 680 units. The earlier Leyland-engined Fleetlines had occasionally run out of fuel on all-day service, so this batch had 204-litre (45-gallon) tanks instead of the 159-litre (35-gallon) version. While the Ailsas had gone a long way towards modernising the double-deck stock at Oldbury and Sutton garages, many of the Leyland-engined Fleetlines wrought a similar transformation at the other North Division ex-Midland Red garages. However, in January 1979 No 6338 was fitted with a Gardner engine, and a conversion plan to phase out the Leyland units was implemented in September 1980. By now Gardner-powered, Stourbridge's 6360 climbs Windmill Hill, Colley Gate, on 29 October 1983. The redesigned front dash panels were fitted to 6341 onwards.

Left: The Local Government Act 1972 had formed a strange area called Sandwell, attaching West Bromwich to Warley (itself a fairly recent creation), Cradley Heath and Old Hill, at the foot of a ridge with surely more in common with Dudley MBC. Residents would need to get to the district offices in West Bromwich, so two cross-Sandwell services were created by amalgamating former Midland Red and West Bromwich Corporation services. These began on 6 June 1976 and represented the first use of the Sandwell 4xx series. The 415 and 417 commenced in West Bromwich and travelled via Oldbury and Blackheath; the 415 then descended Perry Park Road and Waterfall Lane to terminate in Old Hill, but the 417 crossed into Dudley District to serve Halesowen and terminate at Hayley Green, right on the county boundary, with views of the Clent Hills. The servives were worked jointly by the ex-Midland Red garage at Oldbury and the ex-West Bromwich garage in Oak Lane. As usual Alexander-bodied, Midland Red's Fleetlines of 1966-8, forming the DD12 (later D12) class, had been built for operation with conductors, with single entrance door. No 6021 loads in New Road, Halesowen, on 11 October 1977.

Left: The ex-Midland Red DD13 class Fleetlines of 1969-71 were intended from the outset as OMO vehicles and had dual-door Alexander bodies. No 6159 of Oldbury garage works the 201 on Smethwick High Street in August 1976. Its new coat of paint was courtesy of Walsall Works, the paint shop again demonstrating its ability to provide the narrow blue relief band despite the lack of a beading strip, unlike those repainted by Midland Red.

Left: The last buses still carrying Midland Red livery, Fleetlines 6210/3, were repainted blue and cream in the autumn of 1976. No 6210, by now working from Coventry Road garage, is seen on ex-BCT service 60 outside Moor Street station on 24 May 1976. It carries a shade of red briefly imposed by the National Bus Company — darker than Midland Red's traditional colour and soon replaced by the well-known poppy red. This is what happens when blanket instructions are given to freshen the appearance of a vehicle by repainting the lower panels — normally not a problem when there is a colour contrast, but here it looks terrible! The red is apparently the Coventry shade, the nearest the PTE had available.

Right: Quite extraordinary transfers were of three dual-purpose BMMOs — S21s 5849/51 and S22 5903 — to Selly Oak to cover for ailing AEC Swifts on service 27. They ran there from September 1976 until early 1977, 5849 being seen at Cadbury's Bournville factory on 18 October 1976.

Right: Wolverhampton had an interesting miscellaneous fleet of vehicles for physically handicapped children's contracts, while ageing single-deck Fleetlines fulfilled a similar role in Birmingham. The start of a new era came in 1976 with two Ford A-types with 9-seat Dormobile bodies incorporating rear tail-lifts. They were numbered in the bus fleet as 6297/8, the former being seen here in April 1977. They were renumbered 501/2 in the service fleet in 1979 and were followed by 503-18, delivered at the rate of six a year in the period 1979-81. Nos 501-3 constituted the Wolverhampton fleet, while 504-18 facilitated the withdrawal of the single-deck Fleetlines.
Royston Morgan

Right: WMPTE had shown next to no interest in the MCW Metropolitan double-decker, with its thirsty Scania engine, so it came as something of a surprise when MCW converted its 1973 demonstrator, NVP 533M, to single-door (the work entailing repositioning of the staircase) and repainted it blue and cream for WMPTE. The bus, now seating 78, was numbered 6299 and entered service from Miller Street garage in October 1976. We would soon learn that this was part of the development of the Metrobus and gave the PTE the ability to sample a double-decker with air suspension. In 1977 it was repainted silver to celebrate the Silver Jubilee of HM Queen Elizabeth II. The PTE had three further Silver Jubilee buses in the form of new MCW-bodied Fleetlines 6431-3, which entered service in this livery in January 1977 and retained it until March 1978. While the Fleetlines moved around the garages, 6299 stayed at Miller Street, finally returning to MCW in February 1978. *E. V. Trigg / The Transport Museum, Wythall*

Above: Truck manufacturer Foden had built some bus chassis over the years and, being aware of operators' unease at Leyland's dominance of the market, developed its own rear-engined chassis. WMPTE, no doubt finding the Gardner engine appealing, purchased one, No 6300 entering service in August 1977. The bus operated from Liverpool Street garage, largely on the 50 service and its night-time equivalent, the 50N, being seen at the city terminus in High Street on 30 July 1979. Northern Counties, which built the 76-seat body, obviously raided its stock of Greater Manchester PTE fleet-number transfers! Foden did not persevere with the model, and the few that were built remained highly non-standard in the fleets that they joined. No 6300 was taken out of service in 1982 and sold in May 1983 to Goldsmith of Sicklesmere, where it ran for a couple of years before being stood down and ultimately sold for preservation.

Below: The 40 East Lancs-bodied Fleetlines began entering service in March 1977, and delivery would take the rest of the year. Nos 6721-60 accommodated many PTE ideas yet, with their short window bays, looked quite different from the standard Park Royal/MCW design. All were intended for Coventry, but, with the trade union there resisting OPO, Nos 6721-40 began life in Birmingham at Acocks Green garage, still operating its ex-Coventry CVG6s. Coventry really got going with its OPO conversions in 1978, when new Fleetlines, the return of the five Fleetline/Willowbrooks at Dudley since 1975 and receipt of the 20 East Lancs from Acocks Green all added to suitable stock. No 6739 is seen in Winsford Avenue on 9 August 1984.

Above: April 1977 saw the arrival of Leyland Nationals 6801-15. Many went to Selly Oak, replacing short AEC Swifts 3664-74 of 1967, although a little more work was squeezed out of 3673/4 at Oldbury; the remaining short Swift, 3663, had received a pilot overhaul (which determined that the remainder were not worth doing) and was sold in 1978 to Mid-Warwickshire Motors, of Balsall Common. No 6815, however, went to Perry Barr garage where on 18 May 1977 it was photographed in Colmore Circus on peak-hour service 25 (City–Hockley–Kingstanding).

Below: Long AEC Swifts 3675-80 survived a little longer but would be gone by the end of 1977, having lasted barely half as long as the Leyland Tigers they had replaced on the 27 service. No 3678 is seen at Cadbury's Bournville Works in October 1976.

Above: Of the same vintage as the Swifts but much cheaper and simpler, ex-BCT Strachans-bodied Fords 3651-62, new in 1967, were still handling peak-period limited-stop services until replacement in 1977. The 967 (City–Castle Vale, limited-stop) had commenced in June 1972, when these Fords were released upon the double-decking of the Rubery Express (then numbered 99, later 963). The 967 was operated by Miller Street, whose 3656 is seen rushing along St Chad's Queensway on 18 May 1977.

Below: A further 15 Leyland Nationals delivered in 1977 were to 45-seat semi-coach specification to attract private-hire opportunities, but their regular employment was on limited-stop bus services. Nos 6816-30 thus saw off the lightweight Fords. Thirty more Nationals delivered in 1978 were again split between standard 50-seat buses (6836-50) and dual-purpose vehicles (6851-65). Perry Barr's 6860, seen in New Street, Birmingham, on 24 July 1984, is working the Kingstanding Express, for years the preserve of the Fords.

Left: Ex-West Bromwich Daimler CVG6/Metro-Cammell buses had reached Quinton garage by May 1977, when 214H was photographed in Colmore Row on a 9 journey provided by an Outer Circle crew, the Outer Circle being officially the last ex-BCT service with conductors. At Quinton essentially to assist ex-BCT 'Standards' on the Outer Circle, 214H was itself no spring chicken, having entered service in 1958.

GOODBYE TO CONDUCTORS

South Division was determined to lose its BCT 'Standards' at the end of October 1977, when the Outer Circle route was rescheduled for large-capacity buses, including unconverted early Fleetlines 3241-50, ex-West Bromwich CVG6s and similar ex-Coventry buses still at Acocks Green, although the latter had only 60 seats. The end of October 1977 saw the demise of not only the last BCT 'Standards' but the last BMMO D9s. By this time ex-BCT and ex-Walsall Fleetlines were already being withdrawn.

OPO-equipped Fleetlines moved onto the Outer Circle as more became available, and Coventry CVG6s with a reasonable life expectancy returned to their home city, retaining their South Division fleet numbers rather than regaining 'Y' suffixes. The Outer Circle was converted to OPO on 18 March 1978. All ex-BCT services were now converted — a major achievement — but South Division still had a few conductor-worked duties at the ex-Midland Red garage in Sutton Coldfield.

The official withdrawal of the last half-cab buses came at Coventry on 24 August 1979, although three remained licensed until October, by which time the youngest ex-Coventry Daimler CVG6s were 16 years old. The last conductors at Coventry continued until 14 September 1980, while the last conductors of all, in North Division, finished on 13 December 1980.

Right: Following the conversion of the Outer Circle to OPO, the 10 crew-operated Fleetlines of 1962 had little to do. Nos 3241/3/4 went to Coventry, where, of course, the chassis had been built in Daimler's glory days. No 3241 loads in Ironmonger Row on 10 May 1978.

Left: Coventry had its own coach, 407Y, a 1972 Ford R226 with semi-automatic gearbox and Plaxton 49-seat coachwork. Here, on 8 June 1978, it has almost certainly brought Coventry drivers to WMPTE's Summer Lane head office in Birmingham for medicals but does not quite fit into a standard parking bay! It would be withdrawn in June 1979.

Left: Wolverhampton and Coventry each contributed a single Ford Transit to the PTE fleet. Coventry's 408Y dated from 1973, and its Deansgate body seated 12. Pictured at the Sportsman's Arms, Allesley, in August 1979, it looks refreshed by a recent repaint, at which stage it lost its 'Y' suffix. It would run for the PTE until 1981.

Below: The body of 1965 Fleetline 3531 had been burnt out in October 1971, but the chassis was retained for test purposes. In September 1978 it re-entered service at Washwood Heath garage with a new MCW body as bus 5531, looking a bit odd with a 1965 registration. In this view, recorded on 27 August 1981, it has unloaded in Priory Queensway and is about to move to the busy boarding stop in Corporation Street. Service 56 had been introduced as a branch of the 55 in November 1980 and should not be confused with the old 56 in much the same direction to Castle Bromwich, by this time reconfigured (in the extensive changes of November 1975) as the 93/94 (and later 95) to Kingshurst and Chelmsley Wood. No 5531 would be withdrawn in 1982 and sold two years later to a dealer … who scrapped it! Did nobody realise how new its body was?

Above: Astonishingly one of the much-missed Leyland PS2 Tigers of 1950 remained in stock as late as 1983. No 2257 was destined to become a tuition bus in 1971 at the new driver-training school at Perry Barr, there being a modest requirement for drivers with manual-gearbox licences. It was joined by five ex-BCT Daimler and Guy double-deckers with preselector gearboxes. The training fleet was numbered 93-8, 2257 becoming 93. However, it did not really suit as a tuition bus, so Perry Barr's engineers eagerly adopted it as a towing vehicle, in which form it was photographed outside the garage early in 1978. *Royston Morgan*

Below: In the 1970s Leyland's bold vision for the future was represented by the new Titan model, launched amid great fanfare in 1977. WMPTE expressed an interest and received on loan demonstrator FHG 592S, seen in Lower Bull Street, Birmingham, on 10 May 1978. The 93 route, operated by Washwood Heath garage, passed the MCW works and was thus one selected for Metrobus trials. But what did MCW staff think of the Leyland Titan?

Right: The PTA politicians' revenge on British Leyland for its reluctance to supply enough Fleetlines began to be tasted in 1978. WMPTE's future standard bus would be the Birmingham-built MCW Metrobus, of which it would receive 931, almost all with Gardner engines, by the time the bus operation was hived off as West Midlands Travel in 1986. Although the Metrobus body was principally aluminium, the roof frame of the Mk I version was largely thin-section steel, being derived from that of London Transport's DMS Fleetlines and the Scania-based Metropolitans. Initially the Metrobus had two depths of roof structure, the shallower version — by about 40mm — being intended for WMPTE (given its preference for reduced-height Fleetlines), although in the event this remained unique to the first four prototypes, 6831-4. The first entered service in February 1978, the other three following in the summer. They were spread around the garages, 6833 being put through its paces from Dudley. Seen in Hill Street, Birmingham, during June 1979, it demonstrates the brighter shade of blue applied to Metrobuses. The matt-black window surrounds may have been intended to end the need to repaint those awkward areas, but gloss blue was adopted on the production buses. The matt-black skirt panels and stepped cream band echoed features of trendy 1970s cars. Nos 6831-4, plus two Rolls-Royce-engined prototypes (7006/7), had Fleetline-style interiors with PVC seating.

Below: The final Gardner-engined Metrobus prototype, 6835, was exhibited at the October 1978 Motor Show. It had brand-new interior trim, including orange moquette seating throughout, and won the gold award in an international coachwork competition organised by the Institute of British Carriage Automobile Manufacturers. With regular-depth roof, 6835 was the true prototype of the Mk I production vehicle, ordered in increasing quantities by WMPTE — and, contrary to the cynics, moquette seated. The production vehicles started a new series of fleet numbers for double-deckers, beginning at 2001. The two Rolls-Royce-engined Metrobuses entered service in November 1979, at the same time as the first production examples. Nos 7006/7 were allocated initially to Perry Barr and Washwood Heath but later settled at Acocks Green. No 7007 loads in Poplar Road, Solihull, in March 1983.

Left: No 6835 was not the only new type of bus for WMPTE at the October 1978 Show, the first of five Leyland Titans, 7001, having arrived in time to work on the park-and-ride services. Gardner-engined and very advanced, the Titan seated 73 passengers, but, with so much technology, only 26 of these could be accommodated in the lower saloon. The other four Titans, 7002-5, wore different liveries and followed in early 1979. Initially the five were allocated around the system, 7005 being seen departing Coventry's Pool Meadow bus station on 22 August 1979. The PTE had placed orders for 175 Metrobuses (2001-2175) and 135 Titans. However, the integral Titan was constructed by Park Royal, which builder's Fleetline bodies had arrived at a snail's pace, so it was clear that all was not well there, but the PTE was horrified when in July 1979 Leyland decided to call it a day, announcing its intention to close the Park Royal factory. It was obvious the Titans would not be coming any time soon, so the order was cancelled, a further 100 Metrobuses (2176-2275) and 35 Leyland National 2s (7018-52) being taken in their place. The trials across the system having been curtailed, all five Titans were gathered at Birmingham's Perry Barr garage between November 1979 and January 1980.

Below: The last MCW-bodied Fleetlines entered service in January 1979. Of the Park Royal contingent, 6571 onwards had begun to enter service from July 1976, and it took until May 1979 to complete the reduced order for 120 bodies; 6691-6720 had been bodied by MCW in the meantime. Park Royal-bodied 6677 and an ex-Harper Bros Daimler Fleetline/Northern Counties now working for Midland Red load at Cannock bus station on 20 October 1979. In the summer of 1980 a more economic service network was introduced in South Staffordshire, as a result of co-operation between NBC's Market Analysis Project and WMPTE's Field Survey Unit.

Above: Seen working from Selly Oak at Holloway Circus on 14 May 1979, Titan 7002 was given Metrobus-style livery, which in due course was applied to all five. However, with the cancellation of the follow-up order they were left as non-standard buses in the fleet. In 1983 London Transport — by far the largest operator of the type — expressed an interest in them, whereupon they were taken out of service in anticipation of a deal, duly passing to LT in May 1984.

Right: Capturing the October 1978 Motor Show from Earl's Court, London, had been a notable early success for the new National Exhibition Centre. The PTE provided all the shuttle buses to overflow car parks, often some distance away, and this involved a large number of buses. After the Show ended large numbers of older buses found themselves surplus to requirements, and this enabled a start to be made on the premature withdrawal of the 'Jumbo' Fleetlines — the first buses delivered to the PTE, in 1969/70 — whose Park Royal bodies were cracking up, Selly Oak's hard-worked allocation being particularly affected. Helping out at Selly Oak for several months in 1979 were seven ex-Coventry Fleetlines, temporarily banished from their home city by an engineering dispute. South Division, with its customary efficiency, equipped all seven with proper destination blinds. Among the buses in question was well-travelled Willowbrook-bodied 360Y, which had previously run as 1360 from Dudley garage and is seen here rounding Holloway Circus on 14 May 1979. The remaining ex-municipal buses at Coventry finally lost their 'Y' suffixes in November 1979, being renumbered into the 1xxx series, this bus becoming 1360 again.

Right: London Transport started selling its DMS-class Fleetlines in 1979 at only seven years of age. Although LT could not get on with these buses, WMPTE was one of many operators tempted to try them. LT sold them through dealer Ensign, which was prepared to take 'Jumbos' in part-exchange. Ensign also agreed to remove the centre exits and paint them into WMPTE colours before delivery; some of the chassis modifications specific to LT were also removed. No 5501 — the first DMS to arrive, in June 1979 — is seen in Navigation Street, Birmingham, on 5 July. By September 1980 WMPTE had amassed 80 such buses (5500-30/2-80), all with Gardner engines and Metro-Cammell bodies. Twenty went to Selly Oak as 'Jumbo' replacements, while further relief for this garage came at the end of 1979 with the allocation of the first 15 standard Mk I Metrobuses, 2001-15. The DMSs put in several years' good service, finally being withdrawn between 1983 and 1986.

Left: The ex-London Fleetlines were soon fitted with revised destination layouts. No 5558 tackles the awkward right turn into congested Hobs Moat Road from the northern end of Old Lode Lane, on the Solihull/Birmingham boundary, in August 1984. Yardley Wood garage developed a taste for customising its DMS buses: four- (rather than three-) track route-number blinds were fitted, to cope with short workings on the Solihull-area services, while other modifications visible on 5558 include standard PTE trafficators, spotlamps and an angled cutaway above the engine compartment. Many Yardley Wood examples also lost their London sliding vents in favour of standard PTE hoppers, sometimes on the lower deck only — arguably not an improvement!

Right: The ultimate Yardley Wood conversions were 5546 and 5552, which gained standard PTE destination displays, although only three-track number blinds could be accommodated. Seen loading at service 92's Lower Bull Street terminus on 1 August 1983, 5552 was destined for Cranmore Boulevard, Monkspath; in November the 92 would be extended into the new Widney Estate.

Right: The Leyland National factory was capable of turning out far more buses than customers wanted to buy. The powertrain may have been unpopular, but at least it was possible to obtain new buses quickly. Nos 7008-17 replaced an order for 10 Willowbrook-bodied Dennis Dominator double-deckers. Against the advice of the professional officers the PTA had insisted that the cheaper, albeit less-sophisticated Dennis/Willowbrook buses be tried alongside Metrobuses and Titans, but price revision gave the PTE an excuse to cancel them, and the Nationals were obtained quickly instead. They came in all-cream livery in the summer of 1979 and, due to urgent need, entered service so painted; the blue was applied later. No 7016 works the Kingstanding Express in Priory Circus on 27 July 1979.

SAVE ENERGY — USE YOUR LOCAL BUS & TRAIN !!

Left: The initials 'WMPTE' became 'Wumpty' in popular parlance, and after 10 years the PTE acknowledged the truth of the phrase 'If you can't beat 'em, join 'em!' Introduced on its publicity from October 1979, Wumpty was a gnome-like inspector that real inspectors, still suffering comparisons with Blakey in the TV series *On the Buses*, must have detested!

INTO THE SECOND DECADE

The Executive's staff could say goodbye to the 1970s with justifiable satisfaction. They had gone a long way towards the aim of an integrated transport network, the benefits of which were surely apparent to politicians of all persuasions. On the way the PTE had faced awesome problems, notably near-runaway inflation, the dilatory supply of new buses and spares and the terrifying activities of the IRA. The near-elimination of conductors had allowed drivers to receive a better wage that, in turn, had improved the quality of recruits and slowed the drift away from the job. Service reliability was taken for granted by passengers, even in ex-Midland Red areas.

In 1978 Fred Lloyd had been succeeded as Director General of the PTE by James Isaac. Mr Isaac's extensive bus-industry experience was gained largely in the British Electric Traction group, including Midland Red. He rejoined that company in 1969 as Traffic Manager at a very bleak hour and, having helped pull it through, moved across to WMPTE in 1973 as Director of Operations, one of his tasks being to ease the transition of Midland Red staff and bus services transferred to the PTE. Simultaneously tough and courteous, he used his skill and experience to steer the PTE through great changes during the politically unsympathetic period that was to come.

The political climate changed in May 1979 with the election of the Conservative Government led by Margaret Thatcher. She was determined to bring the national economy under control, but in 1980 inflation was still running at 15%, and fuel prices had risen 60% in a year. Two damaging strikes had hit PTE revenue, the 50% New Bus Grant was gradually being phased out, and the County Council grant was half that received in 1976/7. Inevitable fare increases were causing losses of passengers. The resultant massive economy exercise included a 10% cut in services and the loss of 'white collar' jobs.

Love or loathe her, it is clear that public-sector control of public transport was not something of which Margaret Thatcher approved, and WMPTE was one of four operators chosen for investigation in 1981/2 by the Monopolies & Mergers Commission. The 452-page report contained little criticism of WMPTE, which had by far the lowest cost per passenger mile of the operators studied, and concluded that none of the operators was abusing any monopoly or pursuing a course of conduct which operated against the public interest. However, politicians of any party rarely let the facts get in the way of doctrine, and despite the MMC results we were on the road to deregulation and privatisation. A Protected Expenditure Limit was soon imposed which restricted the revenue support each Metropolitan County could provide. The PEL for West Midlands penalised it for its past efficiency, the revenue support for bus and rail amounting to £11.90 per head of population, compared with an average of £29.10 in the other metropolitan counties.

Left: Partial replacement for the cancelled Leyland Titans was provided by 35 Leyland National 2s, delivered in the spring of 1980. These had 'proper' Leyland 680 engines instead of the disastrous fixed-head units of their predecessors, so engineers had great hopes of them. The National was available in two lengths, the PTE having always favoured the longer version, and 30 of the National 2s conformed to this tradition. No 7042 of Stourbridge garage loads at the Rex Cinema, Blackheath, on 25 April 1980.

Right: By the early 1980s Gardner-engined MCW Metrobuses were entering service in considerable numbers, but in 1981 — a time of famine for Gardner engines — the two Rolls-Royce-engined prototypes of 1979 were joined by 20 more Rolls-Royces, 2226-45, allocated to Acocks Green garage. On 17 April No 2239 turns from Stratford Road into School Road, Hall Green, as a Midland Red Leyland Leopard/Willowbrook heads for Birmingham city centre.

Left: Leyland National 2s 7048-52 would be the PTE's only examples of the shorter length, seating 42 instead of the usual 50. They were intended as replacements for the ex-Dial-a-Bus Ford A types, when they wore out. However, 7048-52 never got there, working the 39 City–Witton service from new and transferring to the 101 Centrebus from February 1982. In April 1985 all the Nationals purchased new by the PTE were renumbered into the 1xxx series. No 7049 had thus become 1049 by the time of this July 1985 view in Moor Street Queensway, Birmingham. Because they spent their lives operating in the city centre the Centrebus vehicles were a popular choice for advertisers.

Left: Daimler Fleetlines continued to provide the bulk of bus services. Working from Miller Street garage, ex-BCT Fleetline/Park Royal 3642 of 1967 passes Sutton Coldfield's ex-Midland Red 6283 in Erdington on 26 August 1980. The two garages had effectively swapped work: the 115 (Erdington–Walmley–Falcon Lodge–Sutton Coldfield) service had originally been Sutton local S65, operated by that town's garage, while the 104 took the main road from Sutton to Erdington and onwards to Birmingham city centre, having absorbed Miller Street's ex-BCT tram-replacement service 64 in the rationalisation of this corridor.

Below: After the delays and parts shortages of the 1970s managers were uneasy about depending on one supplier, especially after the Leyland Titan *débâcle*, and in 1980 the PTE tried to order 35 Ailsas alongside 125 more Metrobuses for delivery in the financial year 1981/2. However, the PTA politicians convinced themselves that the Scottish-built Ailsas, with their Swedish Volvo engines, were basically foreign — unlike the Metrobuses, with their German Voith gearboxes — and insisted that all 160 buses should be Metrobuses; these materialised as 2276-2435. To sample what had been missed, the PTE hired this Alexander-bodied Volvo-Ailsa Mk III from Volvo Bus between May and August 1981. In reality Strathclyde PTE A10 (a number it carried in addition to WMPTE's own identification, 7053), it ran in full WMPTE livery alongside existing PTE Ailsas from Oldbury garage, being seen loading in Hill Street, Birmingham, on 10 August. One of the few criticisms of the Monopolies & Mergers Commission investigation was that the PTA should not have interfered in the choice of vehicle supplier — firstly to allow effective competition between them, and secondly to avoid dependency on a single supplier's designs.

Above: A costly experiment was the 600m guided busway in Streetly Road, Short Heath, Birmingham. This was on the 65 route, worked by Miller Street, a direct successor to the tramcar service that had once used the centre reservation here. Opened on 9 October 1984, the busway was intended to prove the technology of unsteered buses operating between steel guide rails, it being estimated that such buses could use 25% less road width than was needed for conventional buses, bringing obvious benefits in congested areas. The route, branded 'Tracline', was worked by a dedicated fleet of 14 guided Metrobuses (8101-14) in a special livery of silver and black, supposedly the colours of PTA 'Chair' Phil Bateman's favourite American-football team; perhaps they looked better on the players than on the buses! These were first used in June 1984 on a contract for the huge International Rotary Convention at the National Exhibition Centre before settling down on the 65, on which they were assisted in the early days by prototype conversion 2686, which retained standard livery. This was also the first large-scale use of electronic destination displays (previously fitted experimentally), as demonstrated by 8108, cruising the guideway in October 1985. Privatisation ensured that the experiment was not pursued, and the guided busway closed in September 1987. Its most enduring legacy was the silver, which, combined with blue rather than black, eventually became West Midlands Travel's principal colour, replacing the familiar blue and cream.

Right: In September 1982 the ex-Midland Red Nationals had 5,000 added to their fleet numbers. No 5139 (formerly 139) canters along Dudley's Dibdale Road, which by 4 January 1984 was gradually being transformed from dismal dereliction into something approaching civilisation.

Above: In April/May 1984 four Nationals, 6844/5/7/9, were converted to 22-seaters, with additional centre door incorporating a wheelchair lift, to work new networks of special services — Easy Rider in Coventry and Easibus in Wolverhampton — for the benefit of the physically handicapped. No 6844 is seen in Broadgate, Coventry, on 3 April 1985, during which month most single-deckers were renumbered into the 1xxx series, 6844 becoming 1844. Another important innovation in 1984 to make life easier for disabled travellers was the addition of tactile plates, with distinctive raised symbols, to the doorways of all buses, so that blind and partially sighted passengers could immediately anticipate the layout of the interior.

Right: In April 1985 Coventry's Easy Rider network received two new Dennis Lancets, 7053/4, soon to be renumbered 1053/4. These were shorter, permitting penetration of certain roads in Coventry not accessible with the converted Nationals. Duple built the 23-seat bodies.

WEST MIDLANDS
PASSENGER TRANSPORT EXECUTIVE

COVENTRY
Easyrider

Facilities for the elderly, handicapped, disabled

COMMENCING TUESDAY 1st MAY 1984

J. STOKES F.C.I.T. Divisional Manager
EAST DIVISION
113-117 HARNALL LANE EAST
COVENTRY CV1 5AD

TRAVEL CENTRE
BUS STATION
POOL MEADOW
COVENTRY TEL. 20014

THE END IS NIGH

A Government White Paper published in 1984 proposed the abolition of road-service licensing outside London. The proposals allowed for any suitably qualified operator to introduce bus services in competition with established services, and for the privatisation of buses. To this end the PTA would be required to give up control of its buses, and the PTE cease to be an operator. Moreover, to ensure competition on equal terms the PTE's successor as operator would no longer be able to cross-subsidise loss-making routes or weak times of the day; these journeys would have to be put out to competitive tender and awarded to the operator requiring the lowest subsidy. The demise of the integrated bus and rail network, built up so carefully since 1969, was inevitable.

In January 1985 WMPTE published its assessment of the proposals. It found the competitive-tendering idea acceptable, but only within a regulated framework that retained the benefits of co-ordination and integration. The Annual Report for the year ending 31 March 1985 summarised the PTE's achievements, recording that it had:

- Maintained overall ridership at mid-1970s levels, arresting a decline between 1980 and 1982
- Invested £120 million on public transport
- Achieved 100% one-person operation
- Introduced and expanded Travelcard, now used by 200,000 holders within the integrated bus and rail fares structure
- Increased local rail travel by over 100% to 24 million passengers per year
- Introduced 35 major bus network improvement schemes
- Introduced 19 centres where bus and train services linked
- Installed 3,500 new passenger shelters
- Built or significantly improved 14 rail stations
- Provided 2,627 free car-parking spaces at 29 rail stations — 89% used daily
- Built five new bus stations with two more on the way
- Encouraged development of locally built buses specifically designed to meet passenger needs
- Introduced special buses for the disabled
- Built or significantly improved 10 bus garages
- Experimented with Dial-a-Bus and the guided busway
- Developed consistent industrial-relations policies
- Introduced comprehensive training and development policies
- Achieved all this with the lowest costs in the country for public transport services in a metropolitan area

Those pleading for the retention of a regulated framework were ignored, and the Transport Act became law on 30 October 1985. Services to be operated without subsidy had to be identified and registered as commercial by 28 February 1986. The PTE was required to form a new bus company to operate these services from Deregulation Day, which was to be 26 October 1986; furthermore the new company, West Midlands Travel, had to be capable of being split into smaller parts, reflecting the Government's desire to sell the industry into private hands. The PTE's operations were thus split into three segments, radiating from central Birmingham, deliberately avoiding the boundaries of the old undertakings, plus a further one covering Coventry.

Many garages were closed in the final run to deregulation, and there were widespread job cuts throughout the organisation. The pain of restructuring was felt most keenly by works staff, whose numbers were reduced by 40%. Works capacity was reduced to the future expected level of operations and acknowledged the reduced maintenance requirements of modern vehicles such as Metrobuses.

The staff of West Midlands Travel and the ongoing PTE went their separate ways from 26 October 1986. The restructured PTE continued with much-revised roles, including identifying public transport needs not met by the commercial network and managing the tendering of socially desirable bus journeys. Thanks to the 1973 Midland Red takeover the integration legacy gave WMT exceptional strength, and, elsewhere, PTE successor operators with a lesser degree of monopoly were forced to split before sale into private hands. The West Midlands PTA, rightly or wrongly, was convinced WMT should remain intact and was successful in this aim.

Left: Nos 2861-2910, entering service between April and December 1985, would be the last Metrobuses placed in service by WMPTE. They were equipped with larger, neater vents as a result of earlier experiments, and many were allocated to Coventry, among them 2891, seen at Pool Meadow on 14 June 1986. Further Metrobuses on order would belong to the West Midlands Travel era.

Right: In March 1984 WMPTE broadened its operations into the coaching market by purchasing Central Coachways of Walsall, which it ran as a separate entity. It also decided to sample minibuses, in the form of 10 Ford Transits with 16-seat bodywork converted by Carlyle. These were originally intended to be 7055-64 and bore registrations B55-64 AOP; indeed, the first was actually delivered as 7055, being seen thus in the car park at the Summer Lane offices on 1 May 1985, displaying a 'WMinilink' fleetname, which did not find favour. Branded 'Shuttlebus' and numbered M1-10, they entered service on 14 October 1985 on new routes in the Pheasey and West Bromwich areas, the legal owner being shown as Central Coachways, which operated them.

Left: Liverpool Street Metrobus 2544 endeavours not to run anybody over during an anti-LRT demonstration at the Council House, Birmingham, on 5 November 1985. A six-mile light-rail route had been proposed from Five Ways under the city centre, emerging at Gosta Green and then running via Saltley and Washwood Heath to Coleshill Road, Hodge Hill. Construction of the final section east of the Fox & Goose would have involved the demolition of good-quality housing, and the residents formed a highly effective action group, mobilising people living further east along the route towards what was undoubtedly the line's ultimate objective, Chelmsley Wood. The scale of the protest finally convinced the PTA that the scheme had failed to win the backing of residents.

Right: In March and April 1986 two experimental batches of single-deckers entered service from Cleveland Road garage, Wolverhampton. Nos 1055-60 were Volvo Citybuses with underfloor engines and 50-seat Alexander bodies, 1056 being seen in Darlington Street on 3 May 1986.

Left: Nos 1061-6 were Gardner-engined Leyland Lynx 48-seaters, the Lynx being Leyland's successor to the mechanically uncertain but otherwise undeniably solid National. With Fleetline 6386 following, 1062 tackles congestion around Queen Square, Wolverhampton, on 3 May 1986.

Below: WMPTE was successful in winning journeys put out to tender in advance of national deregulation by Hereford & Worcester County Council. In addition to services to Bromsgrove, Sundays saw WMPTE buses travelling over the hills and far away on the X92 to Ludlow and Hereford. The Lynxes were transferred for the Bromsgrove services to the garages at Hartshill and Liverpool Street (the latter renamed Birmingham Central during the year), 1062 being seen in Moor Street Queensway on 3 October 1986. The original Lynx livery had been considered so dreadful that they were being repainted as early as May; the Volvo livery lasted just a little longer.

WEST MIDLANDS
PASSENGER TRANSPORT
EXECUTIVE

Sunday, 31st August, 1986

Starting

X92
BIRMINGHAM—HEREFORD
via Kidderminster and Ludlow

**LIMITED STOP SERVICE
SUNDAY ONLY**

In conjunction with Hereford and Worcester County Council.

INFORMATION
☎ 021-236 8313

Head Office: 16 Summer Lane, Birmingham B19 3SD

Above: Most of WMPTE's managers knew they would be transferred to the soon-to-be-privatised West Midlands Travel and that, with deregulation, the bus operations would come under attack from new and established operators. They therefore looked for new opportunities, and on 17 March 1986 the Central Coachways subsidiary commenced a luxury express coach service to London, operated jointly with London Buses and known as London Liner. This competed with National Express, ironically later the owner of West Midlands Travel. Central began the service using two new Bovas, C903/4 JOF, liveried in French blue, but the intended vehicles were three MCW Metroliners with seating for 69, of whom 53 were upstairs. C900 JOF waits at the Colmore Row

loading stop in Birmingham on 30 May 1986. Similar vehicles went to London Buses, and when the latter lost interest in the service West Midlands Travel purchased three of its four examples.

Below: The displaced 49-seat Bovas, C903/4 JOF, joined the general Central Coachways fleet. Partially re-lettered 'Central Liner', they remained available for London Liner relief work. They are seen at the National Exhibition Centre on 14 June 1986. Two months later C904 JOF received dateless registration 245 DOC from an early Fleetline recently retired from driver recruitment.

Above: The summer of 1986 saw several livery experiments in advance of the deregulated era. Timesaver services were to be promoted enthusiastically by West Midlands Travel, and the vehicles appropriately branded. This June 1986 scheme on dual-purpose National 1861 was considered to have insufficient impact, and a silver livery was adopted instead. *D. J. Barber*

Left: Not all dual-purpose Nationals would receive silver Timesaver livery — indeed, a new fleet of Metrobus double-deckers was on its way for such services — so 1829 received the new livery for single-deck buses. This was the newly rebuilt Dudley bus station on 9 August 1986, with buses now loading on the almost level east–west axis; the official opening ceremony was held on 30 September. Route 908 was a weekend and Bank Holiday limited-stop leisure service from Dudley via Himley and Wombourne to Bridgnorth, operated in the summer of 1986.

Right: The front engines of the Ailsas meant that drivers gained access to the cab by a separate door on the offside. This discouraged the changing of the nearside and rear number boxes, so all had been fitted with electronic numbers in 1985. Ailsas 4773-87 had been at Perry Barr since the closure of Sutton Coldfield garage in January 1984, and following the closure in 1986 of Oldbury garage 4738-72 moved to Walsall. In the run-up to the October 1986 handover to West Midlands Travel Perry Barr repainted some of its Ailsas into a pseudo-Metrobus livery. No 4784, seen at Lancaster Circus on 3 October, thus finds itself ready for the new regime.